# Revenue Management

# Revenue Management

## A Path to Increased Profits

### Second Edition

Ronald J. Huefner, CPA, CMA, PhD

*Distinguished Teaching Professor Emeritus*
*University at Buffalo*

**BEP** BUSINESS EXPERT PRESS

*Revenue Management: A Path to Increased Profits, Second Edition*

First published in 2011 by
Business Expert Press, LLC
222 East 46th Street, New York, NY 10017
www.businessexpertpress.com

ISBN-13: 978-1-63157-093-3 (paperback)
ISBN-13: 978-1-63157-094-0 (e-book)

Business Expert Press Managerial Accounting Collection

Collection ISSN: 2152-7113 (print)
Collection ISSN: 2152-7121 (electronic)

Cover and interior design by Exeter Premedia Services Private Ltd., Chennai, India

First edition: 2011
Second edition: 2015

10 9 8 7 6 5 4 3 2 1

Printed in the United States of America.

*To my thousands of students at the University at Buffalo over my 42 years of teaching, who always inspired me to seek and develop new areas of knowledge.*

*And to my wife Marilyn, whose patience and support enabled me to work on this project.*

# Abstract

This book describes the emerging field of revenue management and its applications across a broad spectrum of business activities. It recounts the history and development of revenue management and addresses the analytical tools needed to integrate revenue management into management, in general, and financial and accounting practice, in particular. The book discusses and assesses various pricing practices and other revenue management techniques. It gives particular attention to the role of capacity analysis and the connection of revenue management to the theory of constraints.

Although revenue management originated in the service industry, it is now practiced across a broad spectrum of business and not-for-profit organizations. This book will be a useful guide to managers at all levels who wish to give greater consideration to the importance of revenue management in their organizations.

The second edition reorganizes the presentation of the subject, adds many new examples, and concludes with a chapter on emerging issues.

# Keywords

pricing, revenue analysis, revenue management, yield management

# Contents

# Preface

This book discusses the relatively new topic of revenue management from a general management viewpoint, and particularly brings finance and accounting perspectives to the subject.

Revenue management is a set of techniques to influence customer demand for the products and services of an organization. Differential pricing is a primary revenue management tool. This book explores this emerging field. It describes various types of pricing and other demand-influencing techniques, and suggests approaches to evaluating and managing their effectiveness. Revenue management should be a task of every top executive. Focusing on growing the top line (revenues) is essential to the ultimate success of the bottom line (profits). Familiarity with evaluating proposed revenue management actions and measuring the success of past revenue decisions should be part of the role of financial and accounting managers. This book speaks to both audiences.

Revenue management originated as a specific discipline in the mid-1980s. Its origin is usually credited to American Airlines, which sought to develop pricing approaches to counter the competitive threat of new, low-fare carriers. After meeting its initial goals, revenue management (then known as yield management) continued to serve as a methodology to fill as many unsold seats as possible. These techniques soon spread to other service industries that had characteristics similar to airlines, namely a fixed and perishable service capacity, high fixed costs, and demand that might be influenced by pricing. Revenue management has thrived in these service industries, such as hotels, restaurants, golf courses, theaters, and the like.

Gradually, revenue management has moved beyond the service industries to become a management tool for all types of organizations, both business and not-for-profit. This book provides a guide for managers, in general, and for finance and accounting managers, in particular, to this emerging area of management practice.

# Organization of the Book

Chapter 1 defines revenue management and places it in the structure of management topics, including its relationship to business strategy, marketing, finance, and accounting. Chapter 2 relates the history and development of revenue management and describes several early applications as well as more recent, emerging applications.

Chapter 3 introduces tools for the financial analysis of revenue management decisions, including contribution margin, cost structure, and opportunity costs. Chapters 4 through 6 provide a review of elements of pricing, a variety of revenue management techniques that apply across a wide range of organizations, and findings on the reaction of customers to revenue management techniques.

Chapter 7 discusses additional analytical tools to help implement and evaluate revenue management decisions, including elasticities, in the context of analyzing and evaluating revenue management approaches. Chapter 8 focuses on the critical importance of capacity analysis, applying the Computer Aided Manufacturing-International (CAM-I) capacity model. Chapter 9 discusses the applicability of the theory of constraints to revenue management.

Chapter 10 addresses the relationship of revenue management to providing customer value.

Chapter 11 considers the assessment of customer profitability and the decision to retain customers, and Chapter 12 reviews revenue management decision making.

Finally, Chapter 13 addresses emerging issues in the field of revenue management. A set of references to the broad-ranging revenue management literature follows.

# Acknowledgments

Thanks are due to Ken Merchant, the series editor, for his encouragement and support of this work.

Several individuals read the manuscript and provided many helpful comments.

- Mary Kay Copeland, consultant, corporate trainer, and accounting professor at St. John Fisher College
- Sanford Gunn, retired professor of management accounting and my long-time colleague at the University at Buffalo
- George Kermis, management accounting professor at Canisius College and an experienced lecturer in executive education; and Marguerite Kermis, psychology professor at Canisius College
- James Largay, retired accounting professor at Lehigh University and my long-time coauthor
- Kathy Nesper (University at Buffalo), Eiichiro Suematsu (Saitama University, Japan), Samuel Tiras (now at Indiana University, Indianapolis), and others who have used this material in their classes

Their comments have greatly benefited the book; any remaining deficiencies are mine.

I welcome comments and experiences from readers. Contact me at *rhuefner@buffalo.edu.*

# CHAPTER 1

# What Is Revenue Management and Why Is It Important?

Revenue management has been an area of practice for about 30 years. However, it has made few inroads into the general management literature or particularly into the accounting and finance arena. This book brings together much of the work on revenue management to date and discusses it from a financial analysis perspective. Revenue management should be a part of the focus of any executive; the analysis techniques should be in any financial manager's toolkit.

One common approach to achieving revenue growth is to buy it—that is, via *mergers and acquisitions*. Indeed, revenue growth by acquisition has been the strategy of many companies. Although acquisition is a valid approach, it is not the focus of this book. We consider techniques for revenue growth by building the sales base of the existing organization and measuring the success of that activity.

Revenues are the lifeblood of the organization. Without adequate revenues, an organization cannot cover its costs and sustain itself. Revenues are also the key to organizational growth, by enhancing and expanding the customer base. Thus, a focus on managing the revenue function is critical for organizational success.

The primacy of revenue management is emphasized by Bouter in his recent book, *Pricing: The Third Business Skill*.[1] He identifies the first critical skill for a successful business as creating a product or service, and the second as selling that product or service. The third critical competency is pricing that product or service to achieve sustainable profitability.[2]

# What Is Revenue Management?

Revenue management encompasses differential pricing and other techniques to influence customer demand for an organization's products and services.[3] As discussed in detail in Chapter 2, revenue management began in the airline industry strictly as differential pricing, and then expanded to other industries—initially in the travel and tourism fields—with economic characteristics similar to those of airlines. Eventually, both the techniques employed and the range of industries expanded, to the point where revenue management is now applied in a wide variety of organizations.

Business strategy expert Michael Porter suggests that firms compete in one of two ways: (a) by running a low-cost operation and offering low prices or (b) by *differentiation*, featuring a variety of product and service features that necessarily command higher prices.[4] Walmart and discount airlines fall in the first category; they compete on the basis of low prices but with some limitations as to the quality of merchandise, range of services, amenities, and the like. Brooks Brothers, Mercedes-Benz, and Tiffany are examples of companies that can differentiate their products and services as having superior quality and features. One may describe this framework as *strategic pricing*—the decision by a firm on where to position itself along the low-cost versus product differentiation scale. Within a strategic pricing framework, firms still have the task of establishing and managing the pricing of individual items; this latter task is the realm of revenue management. Thus, revenue management is concerned with optimizing pricing at the operational level.

Economics suggests that, in competitive markets, prices are set by the interplay of supply and demand: Companies do not set prices; the *market* sets them. The stock exchanges are certainly an example; the interplay of buyers and sellers establishes the market price, and potential market participants decide whether they are willing to transact at the specified price. Other auction markets, such as eBay, also operate in this manner. In most business environments, however, the sellers set the price. Even in situations that would seem to be nearly perfectly competitive—the price of gasoline in a community or the price of a gallon of milk at a retail store—we observe variation among sellers, suggesting that revenue management decisions are at work. In some cases, the supply–demand approach to pricing is viewed negatively, as in the case when retailers substantially increase the price of essential products during a hurricane or blizzard. The latter situation suggests that revenue management is not merely an internal function but also one that takes the short-term and long-term reaction of customers into account.

In the long run, prices need to cover costs and provide a satisfactory return on investment. On a day-to-day operational basis, however, many decisions need to be made in pricing, promotions, and product offerings. Revenue management provides the theory and the oversight structure for these activities.

## Pricing and Revenue Management

Price setting is one of the key dimensions of revenue management, with the ultimate objective being profitability. Consider the following three-part relationship:

$$Prices \rightarrow Revenues \rightarrow Profits$$

The linkage between prices and revenues is *volume*. How much can be sold at given prices? Generally, lowering the price will increase volume, though it may or may not increase revenues. Similarly, raising the price will usually decrease volume, but it may or may not decrease revenues. We discuss *price* elasticity, the relationship between price changes and volume changes, in Chapter 7.

The linkage between revenues and profits (income) is *expenses*. What are the costs of generating these revenues? Expenses consider not only the costs related to volume changes—providing more (or less) of one's products or services—but also the direct and indirect costs of the revenue management actions themselves. Discounts, promotions, and other revenue management techniques involve both short- and long-term costs. A significant—and difficult to measure—cost is customer reaction. We discuss customer reactions in Chapter 6.

The revenue management function involves the simultaneous consideration of all three elements: prices, revenues, and profits. Setting prices has become a complex area, one that merits the attention of top management. Price setting should also be on the radar screen of financial managers, who are best positioned to analyze the effects of price changes on profits. Revenue management decisions may have both short- and long-term effects. A decision that appears good in the short term may have negative long-term consequences. Both need to be considered, but assessing long-term effects is more difficult.

## The Role of Marketing

One may ask, "Is revenue management not the role of marketing management?" Certainly, because marketing deals with issues of pricing, promotion, channel selection, product mix, brand management, and the like. Marketing management initiates, and is the expert in, many of the techniques for generating sales. However, the task is not simply to generate more sales. The task is to generate more sales in ways that enhance the current and long-term profitability of the enterprise. At this point, the role of marketing and financial management must be balanced. Financial management must analyze whether revenue enhancement measures will likely be profitable. A look at some of the industries that have been major proponents of revenue management shows the relevance of linking revenue growth to profit growth. The airline industry was the originator of revenue management in the form of differential pricing; yet most firms in that industry chronically struggle with profitability. The automobile industry has also been a heavy user of revenue management techniques. Auto manufacturers and distributors have used rebates, special financing, and other differential pricing tactics as revenue management tools. This industry has similarly struggled historically with profitability. Clearly, knowing how to build sales is only a part of the challenge; one needs to build sales *profitably*. The old humorous saying that "we lose money on every transaction, but we make it up on volume" is applicable here. Although this may sound convincing, it has never been a prescription for success.

## Relation to Cost Management

Cost management has long been a recognized field in accounting and finance. The roots of cost accounting go back to the earliest days of the

Industrial Revolution, as techniques such as product costing and standard cost systems were developed and refined. Cost *accounting* has evolved into cost *management* over the past 25 years as new techniques such as activity-based costing, target costing, and throughput analysis were introduced and gained significant acceptance. Though revenue management deals with the *other half* of the income process, it has received much less attention than cost management.

Cost management has its foundations in industrial engineering and in the pioneering works by major companies. Later techniques tended to come from academics, consultants, and international (especially Japanese) practices. As a result, cost management has become an integrated and significant aspect of financial management. In recent years, cost management has expanded into the concept of *supply chain management*, looking at costs not only within the firm, but also along the entire supply chain from raw materials to finished products to follow-up services and support.

Revenue management had its foundations in the practices of one industry and then spread to other industries with similar economic characteristics. Much of the literature is found in the operations research field, where revenue modeling is common, and in the journals of specialized industries, primarily the travel and hospitality industries. Though revenue management has obvious implications for financial management, its presence, to date, in the accounting and finance literatures is minimal. Revenue management may be viewed as the complement of supply chain management. While the latter involves a firm's interaction with its suppliers, revenue management involves the interactions with customers.

Managing the income-generating processes of the organization is a key task of management, in general, and of financial management, in particular. It requires an understanding of both cost management and revenue management.

## Revenue Growth versus Cost Reduction as a Strategy

Cost management tries to enhance income through cost reductions; revenue management seeks to enhance income through sales growth. Is there a best way to enhance income, both in the short term and in the long term?

The message of the importance of revenue growth has been pro-claimed for many years. A 1996 *USA Today* article reported on a survey of 150 executives of Fortune 1000 companies by Deloitte & Touche.[5] Cost reduction, or reengineering and restructuring, was said to be *out* while getting bigger was *in*. Revenue growth of more than 15 percent annually from 1989 to 1994 was associated with employment growth of 1.6 million jobs, while revenue growth below 5 percent annually was associated with employment declines of 2.9 million jobs. Clearly, revenue growth and cost (employment) reduction did not go together, though it is not clear which was the cause and which was the effect. A 2001 *Wall Street Journal* article observed that one should focus on the value (revenue) created by labor, not just the cost of labor. Companies need to assess the extent to which employees enhance product quality, value, or customer service.[6]

Although this message has been delivered for years, there is still a strong tendency toward cost reduction. In a 2010 *Newsweek* cover story, Professor Jeffrey Pfeffer from Stanford University comes out strongly against layoffs, perhaps the most common form of cost reduction employed by organizations.[7] His lead example relates to the airline indus-try immediately following the attacks of September 11, 2001. Flights were initially suspended, and upon resumption, airlines were faced with con-siderable passenger reluctance and a weak economy. All U.S. airlines but one announced layoffs numbering in the tens of thousands. Southwest Airlines, the only domestic carrier to forgo layoffs, has subsequently suc-ceeded where competitors have faltered. Pfeffer points out that Southwest is "now the largest domestic U.S. airline and has a market capitalization bigger than all its domestic competitors combined."[8]

Professor N. J. Mass from Harvard University found that, even though cost reduction initially seemed more valuable, revenue growth is likely to have a stronger long-term impact.[9] In the short term, the appeal of cost reduction is that nearly 100 percent of the cost savings can drop to the bottom line as improved net income, assuming that cost reduction does not impact sales. Depending on the industry, as little as 7 to 10 percent of enhanced revenue may show up as income, provided that the revenue growth has not come at the expense of prices and profit margins.

Mass notes that in the longer run, there is a limit to cost reduction, and companies can only cut so far. In contrast, revenue improvements tend to compound over time, such that 1 percent of margin improvement achieved through cost reduction is almost equal in value to 1 percent revenue growth that persisted over time. His research further suggests that, over time, one percentage point of revenue growth could enhance firm value as much as 6 to 10 percentage points of margin improvement driven by cost savings.

Empirical market research has tended to support Mass's conclusions about revenue growth. Studies have found that investors react more positively to revenue growth than to cost savings.[10] This response was especially pronounced for growth companies, since investors reacted negatively if revenues declined, even if profits had increased due to cost reductions.[11]

In 2007, prior to the financial meltdown, a *Wall Street Journal* story about Citigroup indicated investors' and analysts' desire for the company to show higher revenue growth.[12] In 2004, Coca-Cola Enterprises attributed its higher profits to revenue management techniques, such as rate increases, contributions from package mix, and volume growth.[13]

Business experiences also bear out the importance of revenue growth and the dangers of cost cutting. In 2007, electronics retailer Circuit City announced that it would cut costs by laying off its 3,400 highest-paid sales associates. Presumably, these individuals were also Circuit City's most experienced and most successful sales personnel. Customers were frustrated to find fewer and less knowledgeable sales personnel in the stores in a business where technical advice and assistance are critical to selling the product. Sales rapidly declined; Circuit City filed for bankruptcy in 2008 and closed all its stores the following year.[14] Clearly, cost cutting failed as a strategy for Circuit City. The impact of the cost cutting was strongly felt by customers, and the impact on revenue was devastating.

Harvard professor Zeynep Ton found that maintaining or expanding retail staffing, even in the face of declining sales, contributed to higher profits. His study of 250 stores over four years found that improvements in making sure merchandise was on display and not in the storeroom, and in returning obsolete goods to suppliers both increased profits. Cutting staff often meant that these tasks were shortchanged.[15]

McKinsey & Company consultants Michael Marn and Robert Rosiello, in a 1992 *Harvard Business Review* article, reported the profit effects of a 1 percent change in each of the four components of operating profit—price, volume, variable cost, and fixed cost—given that other components remained unchanged. Based on average data for over 2,400 companies, they concluded that a 1 percent increase in price (with no volume decrease or cost changes) would have the largest effect, an operating profit improvement of 11.1 percent. A similar decrease in variable cost, on average, would increase operating profit by 7.8 percent. Less effective would be 1 percent growth in volume (yielding a 3.3 percent operating profit increase) and 1 percent decrease in fixed cost (2.3 percent operating profit increase).[16] Their research clearly establishes revenue (price) management as critical to profit improvement.

Michael Treacy, in *Double-Digit Growth: How Great Companies Achieve It—No Matter What*, states that most companies know how to cut costs, but fewer know how to consistently grow revenues.[17] He further points out three key cycles for a company's success. One is *economic*, that is, a growing company tends to have better financial results and lower capital costs. The second is *momentum*, that is, a growing company attracts attention and builds customer confidence. The third is *opportunity*, that is, growth leads to new products, new employment, and higher morale.[18] Companies on the upside of these cycles will usually prosper, whereas those on the downside often decline further. The company that is actively growing its revenue is likely to be on the upside of these cycles, whereas a company focused on cost cutting is more likely to experience declining economic results, slowing momentum, and diminished opportunity and morale. Again, the message is that revenue growth, rather than cost reduction, is the key to long-term success.

Indications from all sources suggest the importance of revenue management, and its likely advantage over cost reduction, in achieving long-term financial success. But revenue management often takes second place to cost cutting as a response to inadequate profits. The most common form of cost cutting is reduction of personnel. As illustrated earlier, both research and anecdotal evidence suggest that cost cutting may give a short-term profit boost, but it can diminish customer service and endanger the company's future. It is critical that the financial executives be aware of and knowledgeable about revenue management techniques to properly guide the company, both in good times and bad.

## Role of Financial Analysis

Financial analysis techniques play an important role in implementing and evaluating revenue management. These techniques help analyze strategies in advance and provide a guide to making efficient decisions with regard to revenue issue: "What is the likely impact on revenues and profits, both short term and long term?" Financial analysis also reports and analyzes the success of revenue management initiatives after implementation: "Were the expected outcomes realized?"

Accounting information is a key source of detailed information for the analysis of revenue management initiatives; data involving various dimensions of each transaction need to be captured at the transaction point.

Various techniques are used to analyze the expected outcomes of revenue management approaches. Such techniques, drawn from management accounting, economics, and other areas, are reviewed in Chapter 3, and are incorporated throughout the book.

## Overview of the Book

Following this introductory chapter, Chapter 2 discusses the origins and development of revenue management, its early applications in a few industries, and its subsequent application in a broader range of contexts. Chapter 3 introduces some of the financial tools needed to analyze revenue management proposals and to help decide if the ensuing growth in revenue will be profitable.

Chapter 4 begins a discussion of the broad field of pricing, the key to revenue management. Chapter 5 discusses and analyzes various revenue management techniques. Chapter 6 explores the field of customer reaction to revenue management.

Chapter 7 presents some additional financial and economic tools for the analysis of revenue management decisions. Chapters 8 and 9 discuss two relatively recent management concepts with special relevance to revenue management. The Computer Aided Manufacturing-International (CAM-I) capacity model, discussed in Chapter 8, integrates an understanding of an organization's capacity and its deployment to the potential for revenue generation. The theory of constraints, explored in Chapter 9, also integrates well with revenue management via the focus on growth of throughput.

Chapter 10 presents the concept of customer value, and Chapter 11 discusses how to determine the value of customers. Chapter 12 summarizes some of the techniques for analyzing and making revenue management decisions, including the role of revenue management in difficult economic times, when pressures for cost reduction often dominate. Chapter 13 concludes exploration of some emerging topics and comments on the future of revenue management.

# CHAPTER 2

# Origins and Applications of Revenue Management

## History of Revenue Management

American Airlines is credited with introducing the practice of revenue management—then known as yield management—in 1985.[1] The first major low-fare airlines, most notably People Express, appeared on the scene, posing a major revenue threat to the established carriers. Matching the low fares across the board was not considered an option because the revenue loss would be too great. American sought ways to target fare reductions to customers, times, and flights in a way that would most heavily impact its new competitors, while maintaining its normal price structure in other circumstances. Customers welcomed the price competition. Many flyers were wary of the new airlines; they appreciated the lower prices but did not particularly want to fly on the unproven airlines. Thus, the targeted price reductions by American tended to keep customers flying American. American's strategy proved successful, since People Express and other new low-fare airlines of that era did not survive for long.

Even though the competitive threat was diminished, yield management survived as a technique because it was seen as a way to enhance revenues, filling what would otherwise be empty seats by offering carefully targeted price reductions. The technique spread to other airlines, and then to other industries with economic characteristics similar to those of airlines, such as hotels, restaurants, and golf courses. Over time, the *yield management* terminology evolved into *revenue management*; the latter terminology generally continues, though some authors now prefer the term *customer-centric pricing*.[2]

# Initial Characteristics for Application
# of Revenue Management

The early literature in the field identified five characteristics that made an industry or firm a good candidate for utilizing revenue management techniques:[3]

- *Relatively fixed capacity*: The inability to easily change one's total capacity or its deployment in response to variations in demand. Airlines, for example, have a given number of aircraft and scheduled flights; hotels have a fixed number of rooms of various types; and restaurants have a given seating and service capacity. Modification of capacity usually cannot be done quickly and tends to be costly. This characteristic by itself is neither distinctive nor restrictive; virtually all organizations have a more or less fixed capacity. If capacity depends primarily on physical assets, short-term change is harder than the case in which capacity depends primarily on personnel. Professional service firms, for example, may be able to adjust capacity via overtime work or temporary staffing.

- *Perishable service capacity*: The ability to sell the services of capacity is short lived; unused capacity cannot be inventoried for future use. A flight departing with empty seats; a night's vacant rooms at a hotel; unfilled space at a restaurant, golf course, or movie theater; and rental cars remaining on the lot all represent permanently lost revenue opportunities. This characteristic generally applies to service industries; product industries usually have the opportunity to inventory unsold products for future sale. However, some physical products may be perishable as well; yesterday's newspaper or expired food products have little or no value.

- *High fixed costs and low variable costs*: Although this characteristic is not inherently necessary, it was common in the early applications of revenue management. If few costs vary with sales, then most of the added revenue from applying differential pricing or other revenue management techniques will fall to the bottom line; the increase in profits will roughly equal the increase in revenues. Assuming such a cost structure was a characteristic of convenience, allowing revenue decisions to be made with little concern for the cost side, because incremental costs were minimal. Consider an airline flight; costs of the aircraft, crew, and ground support services will be unaffected by adding another passenger. There will be a slight increase in fuel usage and the cost of additional on-board refreshments, but little else. Selling a few more tickets at reduced prices will generally contribute to profits, at least in the short term. Minimal incremental costs also apply to renting additional hotel rooms or adding golfers to a course; somewhat higher incremental costs are likely to apply for restaurants and rental cars. But in all cases, costs could be largely ignored since most costs were fixed. Where this characteristic does not exist, revenue management still applies, but greater consideration must be given to the extent that increased revenues will be converted into increased profits.

- *Demand patterns that are uncertain or that vary with time*: If demand is constant across time, it is easier to match capacity with demand. But constant demand is not usually the case; demand varies according to time. An airline may find that its early morning and evening flights are fairly full with business travelers on one-day business trips, but its midday and perhaps its weekend flights are underutilized. Depending on its location, a hotel may have high occupancy during the week and lower occupancy on weekends. A restaurant may have excess dinner capacity before 6:00 p.m. These situations are a fertile ground for revenue management techniques to attract customers to underutilized times by appropriate pricing. Revenue management assumes that some customers are price sensitive and can be induced to shift their business to the underutilized times if the price is attractive.

- *Ability to forecast demand*: Companies that would use revenue management to bring additional customers to underutilized service times need the ability to forecast demand, to identify times when excess service capacity will likely exist. Also needed is the ability to decide which customers should receive lower price offers. The goal is to attract potentially new customers, not to convert existing customers who would otherwise pay full price.

Another characteristic of many early applications was the ability to sell in advance (airlines) or to have early indication of sales via reservations (hotels, restaurants, golf courses, car rental). This characteristic facilitates the ability to forecast demand.

Although these five conditions were common in the early applications of revenue management, they are not restrictive. Three of these conditions are fairly generic: relatively fixed capacity, uncertain or varying demand, and the ability to forecast demand are characteristics of most businesses. Two conditions are more restrictive: (a) a cost structure heavily weighted to fixed costs and (b) perishable *inventory*. These conditions are not inherently necessary, but they do make the analysis of the application easier. Added revenue approximates added profit if variable costs are minimal, and perishable capacity eliminates the consideration of inventory policy. As revenue management has grown in its applicability, companies lacking one or more of the previous conditions have entered the picture.

### Managing Duration and Price of Service

In many of the early applications of revenue management, duration of the service was known or predictable. Air travel, cruises, and movies and other performances are of predictable length. For hotels, car rentals, and hospitals, the basic unit of service is known (a *day*), but the total length may not be. Thus, hotels routinely ask guests, upon check-in, to commit to a departure date, with a possible fee for early departure. Restaurants, golf courses, Internet cafes, and Internet service providers may have customers whose service duration varies. Some restaurant patrons may linger over their dinner and coffee, whereas others finish quickly and depart. Some golfers take longer than others to play the course, or play 9 holes rather than 18. Managing duration has its limitations; golf courses may employ rangers who seek to maintain the flow of play, but restaurants have little control over the lingering customer. Unknown or unpredictable duration hinders the ability of the organization to maximize revenue. Fortunately, few service businesses have significant duration issues, and there is no issue of duration in product-based businesses.

In managing price, one question is whether the same price will apply to all customers at a given time, or whether different customers may be charged different prices. Restaurants, golf courses, and movies and other performances are generally fixed-price businesses, although they may use differential pricing to attract customers to underutilized times. Thus, restaurants will offer happy hours and early-bird specials, matinee prices for movies and shows will be less than evening prices, and golf courses may offer reduced rates for certain days or hours. On the other hand, airlines, cruises, hotels, and, to a lesser extent, rental cars may have concurrent customers who have paid very different prices.

### Customer Reaction to Differential Pricing

Differential pricing has the potential to cause customer dissatisfaction. In most cases, differential prices are presented as *discounts* rather than *premiums* or *surcharges*, because the former is deemed to have much greater acceptability among customers. Some rationale for a price differential is commonly employed, such as an early purchase (airlines), a last-minute purchase (cruises, shows), fewer benefits (nonrefundable airline tickets), or less popular times (early dinner hour, matinee shows). In a product environment, discount coupons and discounts for excess inventories, discontinued products, end-of-season goods, or postseason goods are common. Customer reaction is discussed more fully in Chapter 6.

## Early Applications of Revenue Management

The earliest applications of revenue management tended to be in industries that met the five characteristics discussed earlier: relatively fixed capacity, perishable service capacity, high fixed costs, uncertain or time-variable demand, and ability to forecast.

### Airlines

As noted earlier, the airlines were the earliest reported application. American Airlines initiated yield management to respond to a new competitive threat. It targeted its price reductions on routes and times serviced by its low-fare competitors, with the intent of discouraging customers from shifting. The strategy was successful, and the new entrants did not survive.

After the competitive threat was gone, American Airlines and others continued to use differential pricing, seeing it as a way to build revenue by attracting new, price-sensitive customers. Leisure travelers were the primary target, since leisure travel was deemed far more discretionary than business travel. In an attempt to discourage business travelers from utilizing reduced fares, various conditions were imposed that were perceived as negative to the business traveler. Advance-purchase requirements, as long as 21 days, were imposed, on the grounds that most business travelers did not plan their trips far in advance. Saturday-night stay-overs were another common requirement, again with the thought that business travelers would wish to return home for the weekend. These served as *rate fences*: attempts to attract the discretionary leisure passenger and to exclude the nondiscretionary business traveler. Gradually, however, competitive forces tended to erode these restrictions.

### Hotels

Hotels were also early adopters of revenue management. Hotels have many of the same characteristics as airlines: a fixed capacity, perishable service capacity, high fixed costs relative to variable costs, demand patterns that vary with time, and some ability to forecast demand. Like airlines, large hotel chains had reservation systems that could adjust price quotes based on expected occupancy and closeness to the date of service.

### Restaurants

Restaurants also have many of the basic characteristics that are conducive to revenue management, as just enumerated for hotels. Unlike airlines and hotels, the service duration in a restaurant is variable; some customers may finish quickly, whereas others linger. The restaurant has relatively little control over duration, although the pace of service may be a factor. If a restaurant accepts reservations, it needs to estimate how often tables will turn over and how to configure the availability of tables of differing sizes.[4] Making sure some tables are set aside for walk-ins, especially good customers, and considerations of overbooking also enter into the reservation planning.[5] Many restaurants use revenue management techniques to shift demand to slower times (early-bird specials, weekday discounts or specials, and late-night menu). If food preparation capacity allows, restaurants may also institute take-out service to expand revenue generation beyond its seating capacity.

### Cruise Ships

The cruise ship industry also reflects the initial characteristics for adoption of revenue management. It is subject to many of the same features as airlines and hotels, because service duration is fixed. However, cruise lines typically charge by the person, not by the room (cabin), and have a much greater variety of cabin types than hotels have room types. Cruise lines also commonly sell trip extensions (pre- or post-cruise stays, usually at a port location) and airfare between the customer's home location and the embarkation and disembarkation points.[6] Since airfare may account for 20 percent or more of the total cruise price, one study suggests that attention to negotiating contracts with airlines and selecting the most cost-effective flights may reduce this cost to the cruise line by 5 to 8 percent.[7] In this context, the cruise line needs to be cognizant of revenue management both in its own price setting and in its purchase of airline services.

Cruise ships usually offer discounts on last-minute bookings, to fill otherwise empty space. Airlines, on the other hand, often charge full fare (or higher) to last-minute customers. Why the difference? Airlines' last-minute customers usually have a need to get somewhere on short notice, whereas no one *needs* to take a cruise, a purely leisure activity. Hotels' practices for last-minute customers are likely to vary, depending on an assessment of the customer's alternatives. If there is high demand in the area at the time, discounts are unlikely.

### Golf Courses

Golf courses are perhaps most similar to restaurants, in that capacity is often measured as tee times, which depend on the number of players in a group and the pace of play, similar to the number of people at a table and the duration in a restaurant. Several uncontrollable factors exist, especially weather, as well as the number of daylight hours. Thus, most revenue management applications for golf courses focus on the scheduling of tee times.[8] Opportunities for demand-based pricing exist, usually based on time of day or season.

## Later Applications of Revenue Management

Early applications of revenue management were centered in service industries featuring perishable capacity, with a predominantly fixed-cost structure. When variable costs are relatively very low, emphasis can be placed on maximizing revenue. Most businesses, however, have more than trivial variable costs. Here the emphasis will shift to maximizing gross margin, or revenue minus variable costs.

### Air Cargo

Although air cargo might seem to be a simple extension of passenger airline applications, the situation is considerably more complex. Passenger airlines measure capacity as available seats, but air cargo carriers have to consider weight and volume and possibly product perishability. Passengers are generally time sensitive, wishing to reach their destination with minimal delays; freight shipments may be more time flexible. And although passengers generally represent individual purchases, cargo may involve contracts with shippers for guaranteed space. Cargo demand may also be less predictable than passenger demand. Cargo may be carried on passenger flights as well as freight-only flights. Thus, extending revenue management concepts to air cargo involves a number of additional considerations beyond passenger business.[9] Flight-by-flight pricing is less of a factor than longer-term pricing; and routing alternatives may play a greater role.[10]

### Concerts and Entertainment Events

One-time events, such as an appearance by a performer, present different challenges for revenue management. Capacity is fixed, and demand cannot be shifted to times of excess capacity, since there is often a single performance. Pricing thus becomes especially important. Setting prices too high runs the risk that the event may not sell out, and opportunities for subsequent price adjustments are few. Setting the price too low leaves *money on the table*, as exemplified by resale of tickets in secondary markets.[11]

### Retail

Bain describes the application of revenue management techniques by Tesco, a major British supermarket chain.[12] In retail, the critical dimension of capacity is shelf space; amounts of shelf space and prime locations will be assigned to products producing the greatest total gross margin. And just as airlines, hotels, and other service providers depend on masses of historical data to set their prices, supermarkets also use sales data, including those generated by customer loyalty cards, to make display location decisions.

Pricing decisions are certainly important in retail. Supermarkets and other retailers make extensive use of weekly specials, sales, discounts, coupons, buy-one get-one-free promotions, and the like, in part to entice customers to the store in the first place, and in part to increase the volume of customer purchases.[13] Loyalty cards play a role here as well, since advertised prices are often made available only to cardholders.

The airline or hotel customer usually seeks a single product—a flight or accommodation. The supermarket customer buys a quantity—often a considerable quantity—of products. Some purchases are preplanned, whereas others are made on impulse. Merchandising is far more important in retail, to encourage the purchase of more, and higher-margin, items. Thus, store layout, shelf-space decisions, attractive displays, product linkages (displaying bananas in the cereal aisle), and other revenue management techniques are designed to increase the store's net revenue (gross margin) from a customer's interaction with the store's limited capacity. Tesco's high profitability in a notoriously low-margin business attests to its successful application of revenue management techniques.[14]

## Multiple Service Units

When a single service unit, such as a single flight or one night's hotel stay, is involved, setting differential prices based on expected demand is relatively easy. The price is lower if considerable excess capacity is anticipated and higher if capacity is expected to be more heavily utilized. For many of the business types where revenue management was first used, such as golf courses and restaurants, single service units are the norm. But some business types commonly sell multiple service units in a single transaction. A hotel guest or car rental customer seeks a reservation for several consecutive days; an airline passenger books a round-trip flight, separated in time, with the possibility of multiple flight segments on each of the outbound and return flights. This phenomenon, sometimes referred to as a *network problem*, complicates the pricing. Hotels commonly quote a rate per night; so they can respond by quoting different rates for different nights (e.g., weekdays versus weekends). Car rental companies and airlines typically quote a single price for the package, though increasingly airlines quote the outbound flight separately from the return flight. When modeling is used to quote prices, the models for network situations become complex. Modeling and other decision-making techniques are briefly discussed in Chapter 12.

Beyond the multiple service units (nights) problem faced by hotels is the integration of the varied services that may be provided, such as function space, recreation facilities (such as a golf course), and the like. Hotels must try to balance these various activities in making and pricing commitments. For example, booking function space for a local event may reduce the later prospect of a booking that would combine hotel rooms with function space. Similarly, golf outings might be lost because function space is unavailable, or room bookings by guests seeking golf times may be hindered by booking golf-only customers. A hotel that offers gambling may wish to base its revenue management models primarily on the gambling history of the customer.[15] Integration of all these activities and the establishment of decision rules for advance bookings complicates the revenue management task.[16]

## *Other Applications*

Revenue management is in relatively early stages for many industries. The recent literature has indicated emerging applications in diverse areas such as telecommunications, manufacturing, and hospitals.[17] These applications are likely to continue to expand, because all organizations—even not-for-profits—need to manage their revenues.

# Conclusion

Revenue management had its beginnings in a few industries where fixed and perishable capacity and high fixed costs facilitated the development of pricing approaches to fill as much capacity as possible. As these applications have matured, the concept of revenue management spread to other industries with less restrictive characteristics. Revenue management now has applications across a broad spectrum of industries; the literature reflects this increasing diversity of industry applications. Revenue management is well on its way to taking a place beside cost management as an important managerial task.

# CHAPTER 3

# Introduction to Financial Analysis of Revenue Management Decisions

Management accounting and economics provide many of the tools needed to analyze revenue management proposals. In this chapter, we introduce several concepts and techniques. Chapter 7 provides further discussion.

Revenue management had its beginnings in an environment where added revenue was considered equivalent to added profit. The airline industry, credited as the originator of revenue management, had a cost structure that included substantially all fixed costs. Thus, any increases in revenue from selling seats that would otherwise be empty was deemed to fall almost entirely to the pretax bottom line. Further, the motivation for the initial application of revenue management was not profit growth, but protection from new competition by upstart, low-fare airlines. A secondary motivation was to sell expiring seat capacity at discount prices to incrementally increase revenue.

The early expansion of revenue management techniques usually was found in industries that were characterized by the traditional five *conditions* for the use of revenue management, namely (1) relatively fixed capacity, (2) perishable service capacity, (3) high fixed costs and low variable costs, (4) demand patterns that are uncertain or vary with time, and (5) ability to forecast demand.[1] Given these conditions, increased revenue could still be viewed as approximately equal to increased pretax profit.

As revenue management matures and broadens its applicability to all types of industries, profit considerations need to play a greater role in its literature. While the nominal goal of revenue management is to increase revenues, the real goal is to increase revenues *and* profits. In some cases, profits may be increased by decreasing revenues, but we save that topic for Chapter 12 on customer assessment. Revenues are real and measurable, but profit is an accounting construct, subject to the rules, conventions, assumptions, and alternatives of measuring and allocating costs.

This chapter outlines considerations that are involved in assessing the profit outcomes of revenue management decisions.

## How Is Profit Defined?

Profit can be measured for various purposes, and each purpose typically has its own set of rules and conventions. For purposes of revenue management—with emphasis on the word *management*—the primary concern may not lie with external financial reporting profit or taxable profit. These measures are firm-wide, and are subject to very precise measurement rules. While ultimately we desire that revenue management decisions positively impact firm-wide results, these measures are often not sensitive enough to evaluate decisions at the microlevel. Further, new standards for revenue recognition recently adopted by both the International Accounting Standards Board and the Financial Accounting Standards Board in the United States are likely to complicate the external reporting issues.

Thus, a management accounting concept of profit seems most suitable. Such a measure can be applied on a disaggregated basis, such as product lines or geographical regions, and can incorporate a broad set of measurement tools, as appropriate to the decisions at hand. Such measures help to isolate the effects of particular revenue management decisions.

### When Should Profit Be Assessed?

A profit assessment should be part of the planning and decision analysis stage. This requires estimates of the likely impact of a price concession (or other revenue management techniques) on demand, including its use by existing customers and new customers, the expected future outcomes of such pricing (retention of new customers, customer satisfaction or dissatisfaction, etc.), and the added costs of the decision.

A second profit assessment should occur after the revenue management action has been in place, comparing the actual outcomes to the outcomes anticipated in the decision analysis stage. If the revenue management action is for a limited time, a profit assessment at the end of that time may be adequate, although effects may continue after the promotion is completed. If the revenue management action is ongoing, periodic profit assessments are in order. Postaudit is always relevant as an assessment of past decisions.

## Cost Terminology

As noted earlier, initial applications of revenue management occurred in the airline industry, where the marginal cost of serving an additional customer was negligible. Thus, added revenue was virtually equivalent to added profit. The expansion to other industries where some marginal costs existed, but the cost structure was still largely fixed, did not present great problems, as such costs could either be netted against the added revenue or, in some cases, ignored entirely.

Costs are often classified by their behavior with respect to changes in sales volume. *Variable costs* are those that change proportionately as volume changes, up or down. Thus, a 10 percent increase in sales volume would cause a 10 percent increase in variable costs. *Fixed costs* are those that do not change at all as volume changes, within some range of activity. It is recognized that if volume increases enough, some additional fixed costs, such as facilities, equipment, and personnel, might be required. Increases to fixed costs are typically in fairly large increments—for example, the cost of an additional machine or additional employees—and the resulting cost pattern appears as a series of *steps*. That is, the costs are unchanged for some range of sales activity, then jump to a higher level and remain there for some range of activity, and so on. While the classification of costs as either *variable* or *fixed* is convenient for basic analysis, certainly not all costs behave in these exact manners. The term *mixed cost* is used for a cost that increases as volume increases, but not proportionately. Often, a mixed cost can be decomposed into a fixed component and a variable component.

Another important set of cost terms comes from economics, where costs are classified as *total, average,* or *marginal.* The term *total costs* represents aggregate costs—both fixed and variable—for some level of activity. *Average costs* are total costs divided by the level of activity. *Marginal costs* measures the change in costs for a given change in the level of activity. Marginal costs are commonly employed in decision analysis. In general, average costs are different from marginal costs and should not be used for decisions. When total costs contain a large amount of fixed costs, average costs are particularly misleading as a decision metric.

Assume that a hotel has an average occupancy of 200 rooms per day. Total operating costs for the hotel—building, furnishings, utilities, personnel, insurance, repairs and maintenance, and so on—are determined to be $18,000 per day. The average cost for a room is thus $90 (= $18,000/200). Now suppose an additional 10 rooms are occupied on a given day. Will costs increase by $900 (= 10 × $90)? No. Many of the aforementioned costs will not change as a result of the additional occupancy. To analyze a decision to rent the additional 10 rooms at a discounted price, the relevant question is what will be the marginal cost, not the average cost. The marginal costs are likely to be much less than $90 per room, involving perhaps a few more hours of maids' time, some extra laundry, and consumable supplies. Assume that these costs are estimated to be $15 per room per day. Note that the average cost of a room for that day would fall to $86.43 (= $18,150/210 rooms). The average cost is not a stable number; it is likely to be different at each level of activity.

The terms *variable costs* and *marginal costs* are sometimes used interchangeably, but they are not the same thing. Certainly, marginal costs will include any variable costs, but some fixed costs may be included as well. Suppose a restaurant runs an ad promoting a *restaurant week* special of certain dinners for $20.15, and 100 such dinners are served. The marginal costs will include not only the variable costs connected with the dinners (food, etc.) but also the fixed cost of the ad.

## Cost Structure

Proper analysis of revenue management decisions requires a careful analysis of cost structure to determine the fixed and variable components.

Depending on both the business process involved and the time frame being considered, the same business's cost structure may be different in different settings.

First, as to the business process, the question is, which part of the firm's revenue function is under consideration? If hotel room pricing is the issue, then the relevant costs are those associated with providing overnight accommodations, and not, say, those connected with the restaurant or banquet rooms. Thus, a cost function is needed for each business process; using the firm's overall cost function generally does not suffice. Separating costs by process can be problematical, as one faces the question of how to handle costs that serve multiple functions.

Second, as to time frame, the question is, what is the time period over which the revenue modification is expected? For hotel room pricing, it may be a single night and for airline pricing, a single flight (or pair of flights, including return). The shorter the time frame, the more costs that are fixed and the fewer that are variable. It is said that, in the long run, all costs are variable. Given enough time, any factor of production can be modified. But the shorter the time, the fewer the changes that can be made.

In traditional applications of revenue management, the short time frame gives rise to very few variable costs. An additional passenger may cause a single flight's costs to vary only by a fuel increment and additional refreshment items. An additional overnight guest at a hotel may incur only the costs of maid service, laundry, and consumable room amenities, such as soap and shampoo. An additional restaurant meal will have somewhat higher variable costs, such as the food, drink, and supplies consumed. In each of these cases, personnel costs—often thought of as a variable cost—are probably not affected, since staffing levels for the flight or day would have been decided already.

As the time frame expands, more costs may be deemed variable. If the revenue management proposal involves offering a special seasonal rate, the opportunity exists to adjust staffing levels and possibly other cost elements as well. As more business processes are involved, a broader view of the cost structure is needed. Thus a summer promotion at a hotel may involve not only the accommodations function but the restaurant function as well.

Estimating fixed and variable costs is a very approximate process. Several techniques of varying complexity exist. The simplest, often called *account analysis*, involves classification of each account title as fixed, variable, or mixed (sometimes called semifixed or semivariable). These classifications are judgmental, based on one's knowledge of and beliefs about cost behavior. Another elementary technique is *two-point analysis* (sometimes called high–low analysis), using the change in costs between two different output levels to estimate the fixed and variable components. The change in cost over the change in output quantity would be due to the variable cost items, as we assume no change in fixed costs. Consider the following examples:

- Suppose costs of a business process are $600,000 during a time period when 20,000 units of the product or service are sold, and are $750,000 during a similar-length time period when 27,500 units are sold.
- Costs increased by $150,000 with the 7,500-unit increase in output. This implies a variable cost of $20 per unit (= $150,000/7,500).
- Fixed costs are then estimated at $200,000, by subtracting the total variable costs of $400,000 (= 20,000 × $20) from the total cost of $600,000. The same conclusion is reached if the higher cost-volume level is used.

Using a two-point analysis assumes that the underlying cost structure has not changed between the two periods being analyzed. Moreover, it assumes that cost behavior *outside* the range analyzed does not differ.

The most sophisticated way of estimating the cost structure is the use of *regression analysis*. Several data points of total cost and output are needed, and statistical techniques are used to fit a line to the data points. Once this calculation is done, the logic is similar to the preceding two-point analysis. The *slope* of the line—the rate of change from one point to another—estimates the variable cost component, and the *intercept*—where the line meets the zero-activity point—estimates the fixed costs. Basic regression analysis can be done using *Excel*™. Because multiple data points (presumably over a longer time period) are used in regression, the assumption that the underlying cost structure has not changed becomes more critical.

By whatever means, estimating cost structure leads to an inexact measurement of a moving target. Decisions based on estimates of fixed and variable costs should keep this uncertainty in mind.

A firm offering what amounts to a single product, such as airlines or hotels, has a relatively straightforward cost structure. A multiproduct firm, such as a manufacturer, is harder to analyze, as the cost structure may vary significantly among its several products. Thus, some measure of the product cost is needed. Product costs necessarily involve allocations of many common costs. Costs determined by activity-based costing methods are generally considered the most logical, albeit difficult, cost allocations. However, activity-based costs are long-run average costs, not the marginal costs usually applied in decision analysis. That is, activity-based costs do not tell us what the cost would be at some different level of activity. Also, allocated costs (fixed costs per unit) should not be mistaken for variable costs, despite their per-unit denomination.

In short, no profit measure is possible without a determination of product costs, a process that is notoriously arbitrary and often unreliable. But it is also desirable to avoid becoming too enamored with the accuracy of product costs. For this reason, additional profit analysis tools should be employed.

## Contribution Margin

The common measure used to assess the impact on profits is the *contribution margin*, measured in an *incremental* fashion by assessing the increased revenues minus the increased costs. The standard measure of contribution margin is revenue minus *variable costs*, that is, those costs that change as output (revenue) changes. When we think of contribution margin in an incremental sense, we consider not only the natural increase in variable costs that accompanies the increased volume of activity, but also the possibility that certain fixed costs may also increase, or that new costs may be added to the cost structure. New costs or added fixed costs may not be present in many analyses, but the possibility should be kept in mind.

What justifies the use of contribution margin as a metric is the notion that revenue management generally involves incremental changes to an *existing base of business*. Contribution margin ignores fixed costs, but a business does not succeed unless, over time, its revenues exceed all its costs. Using contribution margin analysis reflects the unstated assumption that a base of business that covers all costs and earns a profit *already exists*, and the proposal at hand is for an incremental change that builds on that base. Thus, revenue management proposals often seek to make relatively small modifications to an existing business base and existing price structure, with the goal of adding to the overall contribution margin of the organization.

Certainly, it is possible to use revenue management as a strategic approach to an entire price structure; in such cases, contribution margin is not the relevant metric. When dealing with the entire business segment, then something closer to full cost profitability should be used.

### Losses from Revenue Management

It is often said that the industries most known for using revenue management—airlines and the automotive industry—have rather dismal profit records. Many airlines operate at a loss, and several have been through the bankruptcy process or have been forced into mergers for economic reasons. Similarly, automobile companies, especially the big-three U.S. manufacturers, have also encountered major financial difficulties in recent years. Because both the airline and auto industries face problems other than revenue—notably an inability to adequately manage their fixed costs—they do not stand as exemplars of the benefits of revenue management. One concern is that many of these companies did not have a profitable base of business to begin with. Another concern is that, as the use of revenue management techniques expanded in these industries, the relevant metric of success may not have changed with it.

American Airlines began revenue management to counter a low-cost, low-fare competitor, by offering low fares on selected competitive routes. When that effort succeeded, the price reductions were continued to reduce the number of unsold seats. These reductions originally carried restrictions, such as advance purchase and Saturday-night-stay requirements designed to appeal only to a small subset of customers. In these contexts, a base of normal-fare business existed that covered fixed costs, allowing the special pricing to be successful as long as it exceeded variable costs (which are minimal on a per-flight basis). Gradually, however, restrictions were eased and low fares spread to more and more ticket purchases. The resulting low fares that exceeded variable costs no longer produced incremental profit because fixed costs were not being covered by nondiscount business.

Similarly, automobile companies began price concessions, such as rebates and low-cost financing, as an occasional price-reduction tool, to move inventory during the slow winter months or at the end of the model year. Occasional reductions worked as long as the company made enough sales at prices that would cover fixed costs. Again, discounted pricing spread and became the basis for more and more of the industry's sales, leading to negative financial outcomes.

The experiences of these two industries provide an important lesson in revenue management. When revenue management strategies are executed, it is important that the price reductions offered do not result in sustained price decreases during high-demand periods.

### Operating Leverage

The concept of operating leverage is a quick way of expressing the cost–revenue relationship. Operating leverage has been defined in several different ways. One common definition is

Operating leverage = total contribution margin/operating income

where total contribution margin is revenue minus total variable costs and operating income is income after all (fixed and variable) operating costs, but without consideration of nonoperating items such as interest expense and income taxes. High operating leverage means that the overall contribution margin is usually well over 100 percent of the operating income, implying a cost structure with heavy fixed costs, low variable costs, and high contribution margin. This scenario is the classic revenue management environment: a business with substantial total fixed costs and low unit variable costs, resulting in a high unit contribution margin. High operating leverage means that the added revenue will have a significant impact on the operating income.

As defined earlier, operating leverage is stated as a percentage or multiple. For example, if the total contribution margin is $100,000 and its operating income is $20,000 (indicating fixed costs of $80,000), the operating leverage is 500 percent or a multiple of 5.0. This means that a 10 percent increase in the total contribution margin would yield a 50 percent increase in the operating income. In this example, the total contribution margin increases to $110,000 and, after the $80,000 of fixed costs, the operating income is $30,000, a 50 percent increase. Note that the current level of operations affects the percentage measure of the operating leverage. At the new level just described—$110,000 contribution and $30,000 operating income—the operating leverage drops to 3.67. If revenue growth continues, operating leverage as a percentage continues to drop. If total contribution rises to $200,000 and fixed costs of $80,000 still suffice to support that amount of business, operating leverage declines to 1.67 (= $200,000/$120,000). Successive measures of operating leverage quickly reveal unwelcome variable cost changes, and show the need to generate increasingly higher revenue levels to obtain the same percentage effect on the net income.

Although often used as a metric, operating leverage is not a particularly useful measure on which to base a decision, as the calculated amount changes over a range of activity. Use of a simple contribution margin may be a better indicator of the impact of a revenue change.

### Reconsidering Fixed Costs

Although the contribution margin is a useful short-term tool, one cannot ignore the fact that fixed costs constitute a very large portion of the cost structure of most companies. Over time, the fixed cost component of doing business has tended to increase. Unless revenues cover all costs, profits will evaporate. Many fixed costs are quite visible—facilities, personnel, technology, and the like. However, some cost factors are more difficult to understand and quantify. One such factor is the cost of *complexity*, which relates to the number of product components, options, or difficulty of manufacturing. An interesting example relates to the automotive industry, which long had offered buyers a myriad of choices, sometimes mind boggling. In the 1980s, Ford was considering how to compete against its then-major competitor, General Motors (GM). Ford concluded that GM seemed to hold all the advantages: greater economies of scale and scope, more vertical integration, more experience, and greater ability to invest in technology. But its major disadvantage was its cost of complexity. The following question was asked: Assume you could produce one car per minute. How long would it take to produce one of each possible combination of options (body type, engine, color, upholstery, sound system, etc.)? The results were stunning.[2]

- Honda, 45 minutes
- Toyota, 24 hours
- Chrysler, 220 years
- Ford, 2,200,000,000 years (2.2 billion years)
- General Motors, 7,800,000,000,000,000 years (7.8 quadrillion years)

GM's apparent advantages were offset by a huge cost of complexity, a cost often not observed in typical accounting reports. The lessons were clear. Today, most automobile manufacturers make most features standard. There are far fewer options and even color choices are limited.

### The Metric for Revenue Management

When revenue management techniques are used to generate incremental sales, contribution margin is a relevant metric. As long as the added revenue exceeds the marginal cost, profit will be enhanced. But marginal analysis works only at the margin. Reduced prices must be limited to a subset of the business, and done in a way that does not encourage more and more customers to seek or expect reduced prices. Tickets for Broadway shows, for example, are fairly expensive. Reduced-price tickets are often made available, at a central location, a few hours before show time. This procedure serves to help fill empty seats, hence providing a contribution to profit. But the short lead time and the uncertainty of whether seats (or good seats) will be available discourages most customers from waiting for the reduced prices to be available. In such situations, the contribution margin remains relevant.

As revenue management techniques become the norm for pricing, however, one cannot rely on the company's fixed costs being covered by *other* business. Achieving a positive contribution margin does not guarantee that a price reduction will add to profits; management must consider costs beyond variable costs and look at the entire profit picture.

## Opportunity Cost

Opportunity cost is an important consideration in revenue management. Opportunity cost is usually defined as the next best alternative's benefit that is forgone when making a decision to do something else. Thus, the opportunity *cost* is the best available *benefit* given up. In considering the revenue management strategy, what alternative opportunities exist that will be forgone by adopting the strategy under consideration?

The concept of opportunity cost is usually attributed to 19th-century economist John Stuart Mill. Scarcity is central to opportunity cost. When there is a limited supply of goods or services to be sold, a limited supply of funds to make purchases, or a limited amount of time to engage in activities, an opportunity cost exists. If there were no scarcity, there would be no opportunity cost.

Opportunity cost is often thought of in financial terms but need not be. An alternate use of one's time, or an alternate use of productive resources, also constitutes an opportunity cost—if we do A, then we cannot do B. In most revenue management applications, opportunity costs are financial in nature. In the common revenue application of offering a seat on a flight at a reduced cost, the opportunity cost is zero if the seat would otherwise remain unsold, or a higher amount if we later could have sold that seat at standard fare. In many revenue management applications, the opportunity cost is unknown at decision time. When selling a vacant seat at a reduced price, we do not know whether a full-fare passenger will later appear and be turned away. In some cases, the opportunity cost is unknowable, even after the fact. If a restaurant offers a special price promotion, it would not know how many customers who took advantage of the special price would have come anyway at normal prices.

Capacity considerations (scarcity) are critical to an assessment of likely opportunity costs. If capacity is likely to be reached, opportunity costs are higher than if excess capacity continues to exist. Airlines routinely limit the seats they make available to customers redeeming frequent flyer credits in an attempt to minimize the chance that they displace a paying passenger. Thus, the two questions to be asked in considering the opportunity cost of a revenue management decision are: (a) What are the chances that price concessions will consume available excess capacity? and (b) how much revenue is likely to be forgone as a result? Even without a capacity constraint, the second question remains relevant: Will new customers be generated, thereby increasing revenues, or will revenues decrease because existing customers take advantage of the price concession? Opportunity costs are present in virtually any decision, but can be especially important for revenue management decisions. The fact that they may be hard or even impossible to quantify does not make them irrelevant.

Consider the case of a rapidly perishable service product, such as a hotel room or a seat on a flight. When the time frame is short for customers to materialize, the ability to estimate the chance of selling the item at the normal price may be fairly high. For products with a longer perishability horizon, such as style goods or a current model year of an automobile, the opportunity cost of selling now at a discount or later at full price is more complex. The time frame for full-price customers to appear is longer, but a current discounted sale may be valued for cash now rather than an uncertain chance of more cash later.

Another application of opportunity costs is found in overbooking strategies. An airline or hotel may overbook to reduce the opportunity cost of unsold capacity due to no-shows. However, a new opportunity cost is created, that of satisfying the displaced customer, which may involve both the immediate accommodation for the customer as well as the longer-run customer satisfaction and retention effects.

Capacity considerations are not limited to physical capacity, but may involve service capability as well. When Groupon was new, it offered limited-time discounts, say to a restaurant or other retailer, and generated a large group of customers. This led to some businesses being overwhelmed by a short-term surge in demand. The quality of service suffered, and both new and old customers were dissatisfied. Revenue may have been temporarily increased, but an opportunity cost in the form of loss of future business may have been incurred.

Thus, opportunity costs are the profits foregone when one decision is made rather than another. A sale at a discounted price has a positive opportunity cost if that sale could have been made at full price. But that sale has no opportunity cost if it would not otherwise have occurred, the business has adequate capacity, and the discounted price at least covers marginal costs.

Opportunity costs do not appear in the accounting records, but they are real nonetheless. Admittedly, it is hard to measure something that didn't happen—that is, "what would have occurred if we did not make this decision"—but this needs to be part of a profit analysis. Revenue management decisions are not free. Management needs to consider the opportunity costs involved, even though estimating these can be a challenge.

## Sunk Costs

Sunk costs are costs already incurred; they cannot be *undone*. Sunk costs include the cost of inventory on hand, costs of fixed assets, and costs of investments. Sunk costs create a psychological barrier to action. We may hesitate to sell a security if its current market price is below what we paid for it. We may hesitate to sell inventory at a loss. Yet economic theory tells us that *sunk costs are irrelevant*. Whatever we do, that cost occurred, which is unchangeable.

Sunk cost considerations apply to markdowns, which often involve selling merchandise below cost. While this is psychologically unappealing, management must consider whether it is better to generate some revenue now, or risk the merchandise continuing to sit on the shelf unsold.

While sunk costs are irrelevant to a markdown decision, or any decision to sell at current (lower) market values, they do have a long-term relevance. Selling below cost has a negative impact on profit. While accepting a loss to move slow-selling merchandise may be appropriate, it also signals a need for better purchasing decisions. The business that has to sell a lot of its products at below-cost, markdown prices will not survive long.

## Conclusion

This chapter considered the role of profit in assessing revenue management decisions. Understanding a company's cost structure is a first step to performing a profitability analysis. Contribution margin analysis is a useful tool for assessment of revenue management decisions, but it must be used with caution. Understanding of opportunity costs and sunk costs is also essential to implementing a successful revenue management application. Consideration of the opportunity cost of a decision is often overlooked. Choosing one path usually precludes following other paths. Analysis of both the revenue management methods chosen and those forgone is appropriate.

# CHAPTER 4

# Setting Prices: An Overview

Pricing is at the heart of revenue management. As noted earlier, we have a three-part relationship:

$$\text{Prices} \rightarrow \text{Revenues} \rightarrow \text{Profits}$$

The linkage between prices and revenues is *volume*, the quantity that can be sold at given prices. The linkage between revenues and profits (income) is *expenses*, the costs of generating these revenues. Thus, we have:

$$(\text{Price} \times \text{Volume}) - (\text{Variable Costs} + \text{Fixed Costs}) = \text{Profit}$$

If the price is set *too high*, the contribution margin (price–variable costs) may be good, but will there be enough volume of sales to cover fixed costs and provide a profit? If the price is set *too low*, volume will increase, but will enough revenue (price × volume) be generated to cover all costs and provide a profit?

The revenue management function involves the simultaneous consideration of all three elements: prices, revenues, and profits. Setting prices has become a complex area, one that merits the attention of both top management and financial managers, who are best able to analyze the income effects of pricing. This chapter provides a brief overview of the approaches to setting prices.

## Types of Prices

There are two basic types of prices: list prices and quoted prices. *List prices* represent announced prices for a given product or service and are often posted for the customer to see. Most retail operations—grocery stores, department stores, gasoline stations, and the like—utilize list prices.

In many cases, there is no opportunity for negotiation from the posted price; the customer chooses to pay the price, or seek the product elsewhere, or forgo purchasing. In some cases, ranging from automobile dealerships to garage sales, the posted price is merely a starting point; negotiation is common, and the final price is typically below the list price. The nature of the business, and customary practices, usually make it clear if prices are negotiable or not. We expect to negotiate the price of a house with the seller, but we do not negotiate the price of a steak with the butcher.

*Quoted prices* are developed for each customer situation, often because the product or service is not standardized but varies in some way from customer to customer. Construction, repair work, professional services, and custom-made products commonly involve quoted prices. Quoted prices may take the form of formal bids, proposals, or informally stated prices.

## Basis for Pricing

There are several approaches to setting prices. Among the common approaches are cost-based pricing, market-based pricing, and value-based pricing.

*Cost-based pricing*, sometimes called cost-plus pricing, develops a price from the cost of providing the goods or services, plus an allowance for covering overhead costs and for profits. An essential element of cost-based pricing is knowing the cost of the item being sold. Product costing is notoriously difficult, as it typically involves the allocation of many common costs. Cost determination is easiest in retail businesses, where the product is usually sold in essentially the same form as it is purchased; hence, the purchase cost is a major component of the product's cost. Cost determination is much more difficult in the case of manufactured products or services, as many cost elements are involved, which typically must be divided among numerous offerings. Having reliable costs is a key to successful cost-based pricing. The development of activity-based costing in the 1980s grew out of company concerns that their cost determination methods were not appropriate.

*Market-based pricing* is based not on one's costs but on the selling prices of others. For commodity goods, accepting the market price is the only choice, as goods are identical and prices are generally well known. In such cases, the seller is said to be a *price taker* rather than a *price setter.* Where product differentiation is minimal (or where one's product is inferior in some way) and there are one or more market leaders, sellers will generally set their prices by reference to prices charged by the leading sellers. Although such products may be priced below the prices of market leaders, there is still considerable room for decision as to how much below the price it should be.

Market-based pricing may be a temporary strategy for a new entrant in a market to build market share. Prices are set below those of competitors to initially attract customers; as the new supplier gains a foothold in the market, it may then be able to command higher prices.

*Value-based pricing* is based on a determination of what a product or service is worth to the customer. Worth may be a function of benefit to the customer (such as a consulting engagement) or a function of how badly a customer wishes to buy something (such as a collectible or a piece of artwork). As a general approach, pure value-based pricing—where each customer is charged according to the value of the goods or services to that customer—is impossible, as there is no way of knowing the customer's value function.[1] Further, such pricing could have serious problems of customer acceptance, as this practice could be viewed as *price gouging.* In most cases, customers have alternatives, and competitive pressures will limit a seller's ability to extract the full customer value, even if known.

But approximations to value-based pricing are certainly possible. Value-based pricing is applied when a supplier creates premium or inferior versions of a product or service. The premium version is designed to sell at a high price, even though it may have a limited market. The inferior version is designed to sell at a low price to very price-sensitive customers who are willing to accept the limitations that make the product inferior to the normal offering. In between, the standard product is sold at a *normal* price, probably accounting for the majority of sales.

At one time, admission to sporting events involved prices that varied by seat location, but did not vary by opponent or the time of the event. In recent years, some teams have introduced value pricing, setting different prices depending on the day of the week, early season versus late season, and the appeal of the opposing team. The Buffalo Sabres of the National

Hockey League, for example, classify games according to opponent, time of year, day of the week, popular rivalries, and the involvement of famous players.[2] Five value levels are provided: platinum, gold, silver, bronze, and value. For the 41 regular season games for 2014–15, 1 is designated as platinum (against the nearby Toronto Maple Leafs on a Saturday evening), 7 as gold, 14 as silver, 11 as bronze, and 8 as value (mostly weeknight games against the least attractive draws). With 5 value categories and 10 seat classifications, as many as 50 different prices apply for admission. Depending on seat location, prices between the value category and the platinum category range between $122 and $240 for the best seats and between $69 and $160 for the fifth best of 10 seat categories.

## Other Pricing Concepts

The preceding section discusses cost, market, or value as a basis for setting prices. Other ways of looking at pricing exist. Holden and Burton, in their book *Pricing with Confidence*, discuss four common pricing strategies:[3]

1. Price to cover costs: In addition to the costing problems just discussed, such prices may be too low (not reflecting customer value) or too high (often because of poor costing or inefficient production).
2. Price to meet the market: *Market* is a collective concept; we sell to customers, not markets, and customers may not behave in a uniform way.
3. Price to close a deal: This approach tends to reduce prices, as customers negotiate for whatever they can, and the sales staff is motivated to respond.
4. Price to gain market share: Employed by firms that are not currently market-share leaders; lowering prices to build market share invites competitors to do the same, reducing revenue for all.

Another strategic view of pricing is the three-way distinction among skimming, neutral, and penetration pricing.[4] These approaches are often linked to the position of the company's product in its life cycle. Skim prices—high prices designed to maximize revenue from the least price-conscious customers—are often used when products are new in the market with little initial competition. New technology items are often priced in this manner, aimed at buyers who are highly motivated to have the latest advances. When Apple introduced the iPhone, it initially carried a relatively high price. It was not long before the price was reduced, to the annoyance of early purchasers. Skim pricing usually has a short life, as competitors enter the market and the initial appeal of the product declines.

Neutral pricing—close to that of the competitors—is usually followed by nonmarket leaders, who will try to compete on dimensions other than price. This pricing approach is also common in stable markets where there is little or no growth, as price reductions are not likely to have much impact on the overall demand.

Penetration pricing—low relative to competition—is often used to build a dominant market position. But as discussed earlier, price is easy for competitors to match, and price-sensitive customers tend to have little loyalty. Penetration pricing works best when the company has built a low-cost operating structure that enables it to be profitable at low-price levels. Southwest Airlines is one example of a company that has followed this approach. Some regional consulting firms have adopted this strategy as well. Regional firms often provide similar consulting expertise to their national counterparts, without the overhead of a national office and facilities in high-profile locations. The low-cost operating structure enables these companies to provide high-end services at midmarket prices.

### The Net, or Pocket, Price

Although the nominal, announced price is critical to the customer and may influence the decision to buy or not, the net price after all adjustments is what impacts the seller's revenue. The net result has been referred to as the *pocket price*. We see one example of this concept in the recent action of many airlines, to quote a low fare while enhancing revenue with numerous additional fees; the pocket price may considerably exceed the stated price. Adjustments in the other direction are also possible, as the pocket price declines from the stated price as a result of discounts, rebates, incentives to buyer or retailer, bonus programs, and other adjustments eroding the net revenue.[5] Many times, these adjustments occur at the individual transaction level, rather than as part of broad price setting. We discuss transaction price management in more detail in Chapter 5.

## Customer-Based Pricing

One of the key elements of revenue management is to find ways to charge different prices to various customers. The purpose is to expand sales by adding customers (and hence revenue) whose willingness to pay might not lead them to buy the company's goods or services at normal prices. The price to each group should be profitable, at least in excess of the variable cost. As will be discussed in Chapter 7, there are limitations of contribution margin pricing, especially where a significant addition to the volume of business is involved.

One of the key objectives of reducing prices for some customers is to limit infringement on normal-price business. There are three dangers to be considered:

1. Different levels of willingness to pay are the typical foundation of customer-based pricing. But assessing willingness to pay is difficult. For example, senior discounts are common. But among seniors, willingness to pay may vary greatly. At best, a company can segment based on average characteristics of a group.
2. Avoiding migration of normal-price customers into a lower-price category, often called *cannibalization*. Definitions of various customer-price groups, sometimes referred to as *rate fences*, are needed to try to control this danger. At best, any solutions will be imperfect.
3. Discouraging third-party resellers, who might find ways to buy at low prices and resell at somewhat higher prices to those who did not qualify for the lower prices. This process is often called *arbitrage.*

Unless these dangers can be controlled, customer-based pricing has the potential to result in a general lowering of prices for nearly all customers, which usually means a reduction of profitability. There are numerous approaches to customer-based pricing, as described in the following sections.[6]

### Customer Groups

A common approach to customer-based pricing is to define one or more groups that qualify for a lower price. Perhaps, the most common group is *senior citizens*; the group may be defined by a minimum age, which varies across establishments from perhaps 55 to 65 years. Alternatively, membership in a senior-related organization, such as the American Association of Retired Persons (now simply known as AARP), may be the qualifier. The assumption, certainly not always valid, is that seniors have lower incomes and a lower willingness to pay.

Other groups that may be offered lower prices include students, members of the military, and clergy. Members of certain organizations, such as the American Automobile Association (AAA) and the aforementioned AARP, may receive special pricing.

At the business level, repeat customers, customers who buy large quantities, or customers that are not-for-profit organizations may qualify for discounts. In these cases, the seller typically establishes criteria for qualifiers.

### Discount Times

Rather than extending price reductions to all members of a group, discounted prices may be based on some element of time. *Time* may refer to underutilized portions of the day, week, or year; the seasonal cycle of the product or service; advance commitment; or speed of delivery. The following are some examples:

- *Slow-time pricing*: *Early bird specials* at restaurants, matinee performances for films or shows, weekend rates at business hotels, and off-season rates at resorts.
- *End-of-season pricing*: Closeouts of seasonal merchandise such as clothing, lawn mowers, and outdoor furniture; end-of-model year discounts on automobiles; postholiday sales of holiday-related merchandise.
- *Preseason pricing*: Back-to-school sales, summertime maintenance of heating systems.

- *Advance-purchase pricing*: Early reservation prices for cruises, prepublication prices for a specialty book.
- *Speed-of-delivery pricing*: One-hour dry cleaning, overnight shipping (these would command premium, rather than discount, pricing).

### Location-Based Pricing

Prices may vary based on the location where goods and services are offered. Rather than discounts, items may sell at a premium in certain locations. Gifts and souvenirs may be priced higher in an airport shop than in a downtown store. A beer may cost more at a sporting event than at the corner bar. A gallon of milk may cost more in a convenience store than in a supermarket. Many items sell for more in Hawaii than on the mainland.

In some cases, price differentials may be based on the cost of doing business, as some locations are costlier than others. In other cases, higher prices may be extracted from a captive audience that has few alternatives, as in the case of the sporting events and the airport shops just mentioned.

### Product Variations

Another strategy to enable price variation among customers is to offer variations of one's product or service, even if the variations are more apparent than real.

Many manufacturers of branded products produce highly similar versions that are sold under private label or as generic brands at a lower price. This practice is perhaps one of the most effective means of adding customers with a lower willingness to pay while largely protecting normal-price business. Highly price-sensitive customers will tend to shop at locations carrying off-brands and generics, whereas less price-sensitive customers will shop at mainstream stores and are likely to continue to buy their familiar brands.

In other cases, all items will carry the brand name but a number of versions will be available. Technology items—computers, peripherals, digital cameras, smartphones, software products, and the like—will have a variety of included features so as to create a range of prices, appealing to both the price-sensitive bare-bones buyer and the buyer who must have the top-of-the-line version, whatever the price. It is likely that production cost variations from the bottom to the top of the line are far less than the price variations. Sometimes model numbers will differ between products offered online and products offered in retail stores, making price comparison difficult.

The opposite of the private-label strategy is the establishment of premium brands at higher prices. One advantage of this approach is that the premium brand might generate higher revenue from prestige-seeking, non-price-sensitive customers. Another advantage is that the existence of a high-priced premium brand may make the normal-priced standard brand seem less expensive and a better buy.

Product variation is probably the most common means of revenue management. Companies create a variety of goods and services to appeal to a wide range of customer desires and willingness to pay. Most customers welcome the variety of choices available to them, while others feel that buying decisions are unduly complicated. When Medicare Part D, the prescription drug benefit, was introduced, so many plans were made available by varying suppliers, each offering slightly different coverage at different prices that consumers (primarily seniors) found it extremely hard to select.

### Variation by Distribution Channel

Prices may vary depending on where the transaction is conducted. Goods may be bought at normal retail locations, at outlet stores, via catalog, or online. Often, price differences reflect true cost differences. It is clearly more expensive to operate, staff, and stock retail space than to offer goods over the Internet. Customer service also varies across different types of outlets, so that price-sensitive customers can trade off some degree of service and convenience for lower prices. Customers willing to navigate a sometimes-complex Internet site and ordering process may find lower prices and possibly greater selection than at a local retailer.

Similarly, customers willing to go to a less conveniently located outlet store may find lower prices than those at their local mall. Typically, outlet stores were located in more remote areas, far from a company's full-price stores. Recently, that trend is changing, as outlet stores are appearing in major cities and full-price stores are coming to outlet malls. There is debate as to whether this trend will have positive or negative effects. Proponents suggest that there is little overlap in customer groups between outlet and full-price stores, and that improving access to outlet stores will enhance overall revenues. Opponents suggest that increased proximity will draw customers away from full-price stores and depress overall revenues.[7]

### Customer Option

In some cases, price reductions are offered to customers willing to endure minor additional efforts, such as redeeming coupons and submitting rebate claims. Buyers may choose to avail themselves of these reductions or not.

### Summary of Customer-Based Pricing

Most companies, in fact, offer customer-based pricing, using one or more of the techniques just described. Finding ways to charge different prices to different customers is easy. The following are the two important questions for successful revenue management:

1. Does the technique used enhance both revenue and profit, especially over the long run?
2. How do customers react—positively or negatively—to the price differences?

We further discuss the first question at the end of this chapter; customer response is addressed in Chapter 6.

## Auction-Based Pricing

The emergence of Priceline, eBay, and other online transaction sites has expanded the use of auction-based pricing. Once used primarily for quick disposal of merchandise, often under distress conditions, auctions are now much more widely used. In an auction, the seller accepts the price of the highest bidder, although the seller may set an undisclosed minimum price, known as a *reserve price*. Auction is a form of value pricing, where the competition among potential buyers for a limited supply—often a single item—establishes the value. The success of auction-based pricing depends on achieving broad awareness of the sale and attracting a sufficient number of interested buyers.

Some forms of auction sales, such as those by Priceline, feature the traditional practitioners of revenue management—airlines, hotels, car rental agencies, and the like. The online auction provides another means of filling perishable capacity. Bids are generally not visible to other customers, as they are on eBay, and the reserve price is typically not fixed. This type of auction is intended for use on an ongoing basis, with a continuing supply of products for sale.

Other forms of auction sales, such as those on eBay, are more used for infrequent or one-time sales of small quantities, sometimes a single item. Bids are by necessity visible to other bidders, as they would be in a live auction. Although a live auction continues until only a single bidder remains, online auctions usually have a time limit.

### Competitive Bidding

Another form of auction sale, though that term is typically not used, occurs when buyers solicit bids for goods or services. Here the seller, rather than the buyer, makes the bid. In a standard auction, the buyer making the high bid wins; in a competitive bidding auction, the seller making the low bid wins. Many construction contracts are awarded on a competitive bid basis, as are some contracts for the supply of certain standard goods over a period of time. The buyer's requirements are often complex, set forth as *specifications* to be met. Bids are *sealed*, not visible to other bidders or even to the buyer until the bidding period ends and bids are *opened*. A good deal of government procurement is done on an *auction* basis; many governmental entities require competitive bidding for certain purchases.

Pricing in a competitive bidding environment involves a combination of cost-based and market-based pricing. The bid needs to be cost based, in that the bidder will typically wish to quote a price that covers costs and earns some profit. But it also needs to be market based, assessing what other suppliers are likely to bid. Only one award will typically be made, to the lowest bidder who satisfies the quoted specifications. Ideally, one seeks to be the low bidder, but not too much below the second lowest. This type of pricing requires considerable skill.

## Applicability of Revenue Management

Revenue management is most associated with customer-based pricing, finding ways to increase total revenue and profit by attracting more customers by offering differential pricing in some form. Yet, revenue management, in the sense of analyzing pricing decisions in accounting and finance terms, applies to all forms of pricing: whether setting list prices or establishing quoted prices for individual customers, and whether prices are based on costs, market conditions, or perceptions of value to the customer. Revenue management using customer-based techniques is not without risks. It must be evaluated to determine that the increased revenues will increase profitability in both the short and long terms. This requires careful analysis and ongoing monitoring.

# CHAPTER 5

# Revenue Management Techniques

Companies seeking to manage their revenue function may use a variety of techniques to accomplish their goal of increased revenue with sustainable profit improvement. This chapter discusses several of these approaches:

- Sale or promotional pricing (discounting)
- Price matching
- Markdowns
- Unlimited-use pricing
- Overbooking
- Bundling and unbundling
- Free as a price
- Customer reward programs

## Sale or Promotional Pricing (or Discounting)

Discounting is probably the most widely used revenue management technique. In general, a discount is a temporary price reduction available to all customers. Sometimes called a *sale* or a *special promotion*, discounting seeks to stimulate demand for a period of time. At the end of the discount period, prices will return to their normal levels. This characteristic distinguishes a *discount* from a *markdown*, which is discussed later.

A discount is generally available to all customers during the discount period. Customer-based pricing, discussed in the preceding chapter, limits the price reduction to certain customers or customer classes (e.g., a senior discount), although the term *discount* is used in this context as well. Further, while discounting is generally a limited-time practice, customer-based prices such as senior discounts tend to be permanent.

The remainder of this section discusses discounting in the context of temporary price reductions available to all customers.

In retail, a sale or promotion—such as *buy one, get one free*—is a limited-time price reduction. It may be used to stimulate demand during slow periods, such as postholiday sales or the once-common *January white sales* for dry goods. One key to success for this technique is infrequency; businesses that seem to always have a sale, train their customers that the sale price is the normal price. That may indeed be the company's intent, and it uses sales simply as an advertising technique. But if a company expects to sell its products at normal prices during nonsale times, it cannot have sales too frequently. Sears' appliance business suffered from this problem. If customers didn't need to purchase an appliance today, they knew that a sale would be forthcoming and thus they should wait—usually only a few weeks—to make their purchase. Sears recognized this impact and attempted to switch to an *everyday low price* format. The attempt was unsuccessful because Sears had trained its customers too well to wait for a sale. The automobile business, in recent years, has fallen into this same pattern, with a succession of rebates, low-cost financing, and other incentives. A given promotion may expire at the end of the current month, but customers know that another promotion will occur next month. Thus, the danger to be avoided with sale pricing is the destruction of regular-price business. Sales should be infrequent and of relatively short duration, ideally to stimulate demand during normally slow times, lest the sale price become the regular price.

Some retailers, such as Walmart and *dollar stores*, successfully avoid the dangers of sale pricing by rigorous adherence to an everyday-low-pricing strategy. Price reductions designated as *rollbacks* may occur, but they are not positioned as limited-time sales. Few businesses have the discipline to successfully maintain an everyday-low-price strategy. Businesses such as Sears and JC Penney that have tried to change from a discounting strategy to an everyday-low-price strategy have generally not been successful.

Some discounts are offered for very brief time periods but on a regular basis, at times when there is low demand. Examples include early-bird specials at a restaurant, happy hour at a bar, weekend rates at a downtown hotel, or matinee pricing at a theater. The goal here is to shift some demand from high-utilization times (when demand may exceed capacity) to low-utilization times, or to increase total demand by appealing to price-sensitive customers who would not patronize the establishment at regular prices. To be financially viable, such promotions must cover marginal costs and not excessively cannibalize full-price business.

Not all discounting occurs during times of low demand. *Black Friday* (the day after Thanksgiving in the United States) is a notoriously busy shopping day; yet many retailers offer seemingly substantial discounts to lure shoppers to their establishments. However, one study has suggested that Black Friday discounts are more apparent than real. Retailers and suppliers work together to plan pricing and discounts that will still yield desired profit margins. The study of 31 major retailers found that, between 2009 and 2012, 63 percent more discount deals were offered, and average discounts increased from 25 percent to 36 percent, but gross margins stayed constant at 27.9 percent.[1]

In businesses where price negotiation between buyers and sellers is common, discounting is a frequent, though not necessarily productive, technique. In this context, though a discount is potentially available to all buyers, the amount varies according to the buyer's negotiating skill and the seller's desperation to make a sale. Discounting begins from an initially quoted price and moves lower, sometimes aided by the buyer playing one competitor against another. Discounting is often a losing game for the seller, as frequent bidding wars lead to a *death spiral* situation where all sellers lose (though buyers win) and prices may be continuously too low to be profitable. One author argues that "if all you talk about with customers is price, there is no price that is going to be low enough."[2] Discounting tends to be a poor way of building revenue growth because profits may disappear as a result.

The profit impact of discounting depends heavily on the firm's cost structure. Consider two firms, whose current situations are shown in Table 5.1.

Each firm believes that a 10 percent price reduction will increase sales volume by 18 percent. If the price reduction is implemented and the expected sales growth occurs, the new profit levels would be those shown in Table 5.2.

As can be seen, the price reduction benefited firm 1, whose high operating leverage generated a positive return from the added sales; profits

*Table 5.1 Initial profit data for two firms*

|  | Firm 1 ($) | Firm 2 ($) |
|---|---|---|
| Revenues (each selling 10,000 units at $10 each) | 100,000 | 100,000 |
| Variable costs ($2 per unit for firm 1, and $7 per unit for firm 2) | (20,000) | (70,000) |
| Fixed costs | (70,000) | (20,000) |
| Profit | 10,000 | 10,000 |

*Table 5.2 Profits after discounting*

|  | Firm 1 ($) | Firm 2 ($) |
|---|---|---|
| Revenues (each selling 11,800 units at $9 each) | 106,200 | 106,200 |
| Variable costs ($2 per unit for firm 1, and $7 per unit for firm 2) | (23,600) | (82,600) |
| Fixed costs | (70,000) | (20,000) |
| Profit | 12,600 | 3,600 |

increased by over 25 percent. The opposite held for firm 2, where the increased sales were not enough to overcome the sizable reduction in its contribution margin, and profits fell by nearly two-thirds. This simple illustration shows that, although discounting may increase sales, analysis is needed to see if that increase is likely to be both sustainable and profitable.

## Price Matching

Some businesses employ a selective form of discounting known as *price matching*. The business offers to meet competitive prices, usually with conditions attached. Conditions may include the price being for the *same product* and offered by a competitor within a specified geographical distance. Prior sales are generally excluded. However, application is difficult and sometimes arbitrary. Determining that the item in question is the *same product* may be difficult, as some retailers carry exclusive versions. This is especially true for electronic goods, where model numbers for apparently identical products may vary from one retailer to another.[3]

    Sometimes, the offer of price matching carries problems for a retailer. In one reported instance, Dollar General advertised a $9.50 sale price for *all counts and sizes* of a brand-name diaper. The products come in about 40 different packages of diaper sizes and counts. Dollar General carried only smaller-count packages, and its discount amounted to about $0.50 per pack. But the ad said *all counts and sizes*; so shoppers went to retailers who promised to match competitor prices, such as Wal-Mart, Target, and Toys 'R' Us, and asked to have the price matched on the much larger packages they carried. On large packages, the $9.50 price involved a discount of $20 or more. News of this opportunity spread quickly via social media. After a few days, the large retailers stopped honoring the price match. This, in turn, caused a good deal of customer unhappiness and complaint.[4]

Price matching is a difficult strategy to implement successfully. As the above anecdote illustrates, the need to exactly match the competitor's offer may cause dissatisfaction when customers' matching requests are not honored. Further, decisions to honor or not honor a competitor price tend to slow down customers checkout lines. Price matching may have more pitfalls than benefits as a revenue management technique.

Third-party price matching also exists. Some credit card companies offer *price protection*, refunding the difference if a customer buys an item and later finds it cheaper. Numerous limitations and conditions typically exist, such as a dollar maximum, the exclusion of certain purchases, time limits, and requirements for documentation. It seems likely that successful claims are rare.

## Markdowns

Unlike the temporary price reductions of sales or promotions, markdowns represent permanent reductions in the price of the affected goods. Markdowns are most commonly used for holiday-related items after the holiday is past, for end-of-season apparel and other items, and for end-of-model-year items, such as automobiles. The stock of items available at markdown prices is limited and will not be replenished.

Some retailers, however, employ markdowns as an ongoing pricing technique, reducing the price if the merchandise has been on hand beyond a certain time. The key revenue management decisions include how much to reduce the price and how soon to do it. Markdowns exist in a wide range of products. Houses on the resale market are typically reduced in asking price if, after some time, they have not sold at the originally listed price. Supermarkets reduce day-old baked goods as well as other soon-to-expire merchandise. Style goods are often marked down fairly quickly. If a particular style doesn't sell well initially, it is not likely to sell well later; the price is reduced, sometimes in steps, to move the merchandise. Markdowns have grown over time. A somewhat-dated study reported that markdowns represented 6.1 percent of department store sales in 1965, 8.9 percent in 1975, and 18 percent in 1984; by the mid-1990s, only 20 percent of the merchandise in a typical department store was sold at full price.[5] Markdowns are not limited to department stores; looking across the retail spectrum—clothing, electronics, toys, and the like—marked-down goods represented 33 percent of sales in 2001.[6]

Markdowns are an established revenue management strategy, though not always by that name. The earliest applications of revenue management by airlines and hotels were essentially markdowns (and sometimes markups) to fill available seats or rooms before they *perished*. Even in cases where prices are commonly subject to negotiation, as in automobiles and houses, the asking price initially attracts or repels potential customers. Thus, markdowns to the asking price, as in the house on the market for some time, may bring new potential buyers to the seller.

## Unlimited Use (All-You-Can-Eat) Pricing

This strategy involves offering a product or service in unlimited quantity, typically over a fixed time period. Although we may think of this strategy primarily in the context of restaurants, this pricing type is employed by many businesses, for varying reasons:

- Transportation providers may offer a one-price, unlimited-use pass. Bus and rail companies routinely offer such passes as a convenience and inducement to regular riders. Occasionally, airlines offer a limited-time, all-you-can-fly price, usually to build additional demand during normally slow times. A few years ago, JetBlue Airways offered a one-month pass at two prices: $699 to fly on any available flight between

September 7 and October 6, or $499 to fly any day but Friday or Sunday.[7] Whether offering an unlimited-use pass is an effective revenue management strategy depends on whether it attracts new business, or simply causes passengers who had already planned multiple trips in that time frame to switch to a cheaper option. One cash flow advantage is that such passes are typically bought and paid for further in advance of usage than normal airline tickets.

- Theme parks, museums, sports teams, and other attractions often offer a season pass in lieu of individually charged admissions. Again, the season pass is intended as a convenience and inducement to regular attendees. Having a base of season customers may serve to reduce marketing costs and provide earlier cash flow. Where ancillary revenues are important, such as concessions at a sporting event, they may offset lower admission prices. Furthermore, having an annual pass may cause holders to attend more frequently than if they were to purchase individual admissions. Disney World, for example, currently (2014) offers daily adult admission for $99 and an annual pass for $634. Florida residents may buy annual passes at prices ranging from $190.64 to $644.33, depending on what is included (parking, weekdays only, after 4:00 p.m. only, etc.). These reduced prices might encourage Florida residents to frequent the parks for shopping or dining, sources of significant ancillary revenues. They might also encourage residents to bring their out-of-town guests to Disney World.

- Telephone, Internet, and cable providers commonly charge a fixed price for unlimited service, perhaps primarily for billing convenience and to avoid the cost of monitoring usage (which in some cases may not even be possible). This approach to pricing ensures a steady revenue stream even if utilization declines, with the option of increasing the price if utilization increases.

Analysis of such pricing schemes is difficult because the degree of expected utilization is unknown. Generally, this type of pricing would be found in businesses with high fixed costs and a fair amount of excess capacity.

Unlimited use pricing sometimes leads to abuse by customers. Some wireless and Internet providers find excessive downloading of high-volume content by some customers, necessitating limits on *unlimited* use.

## Overbooking

Businesses that operate by advance reservation recognize that some reservations will not be fulfilled. In the face of sufficient demand, and with a desire to not have unutilized capacity, such businesses may accept more reservations than capacity allows. If the business is successful in estimating the frequency of no-shows, this process enhances revenue with minimal adverse customer effects. If, however, the estimate of no-shows is too high, this practice may become more costly than beneficial. Costs involve both the remedy offered to the customer and the effects of customer unhappiness with not receiving the expected service.

Airlines face the most complex situation. The capacity on a flight is absolutely limited, and an alternative flight may not be available for several hours, sometimes longer. By both company policy and federal regulations, airlines have a protocol to follow in the face of overbooking. Volunteers are first sought who will give up their seat on the flight in question in exchange for a seat on a later flight plus a payment, often in the form of a voucher for a future flight. Customers who have time flexibility sometimes welcome these opportunities. If sufficient volunteers cannot be found, then passengers holding reservations may be involuntarily *bumped* from the flight, again with specified compensation. Not only is the bumping compensation higher than what might be offered to volunteers, the bumping process may result in very unhappy customers, who may choose to patronize a different airline in the future.

Hotels face somewhat less complex situations. Even though a hotel is *full*, it may have a few rooms that have minor service problems or are held for special situations that could be utilized for overbooked customers. A rate reduction, or an upgrade to an unoccupied suite, may minimize customer dissatisfaction. If there is literally no space, the response of the hotel is typically to find the customer a room in a nearby facility, a process known as *walking*. Even though this solution somewhat inconveniences the customer, it is far less so than the bumped airline passengers who will not reach their destination when desired.

Overbooking by a restaurant may simply involve a longer wait to be seated. Since the duration of restaurant service varies, customers understand that their table may not be ready at the time specified. A modest wait is unlikely to have serious consequences, though a long wait could cause loss of future business.

The concept of *overbooking* is not limited to fixed-capacity service businesses such as those discussed earlier. Any business can *overbook* in the sense of promising customers what it is then unable to deliver. A retailer offering a sale price on an item of merchandise may not have sufficient stock to meet the demand. A common response is the issuance of a *rain check*, enabling the customer to buy the item, at the sale price, when stock is replenished. For some sales, such as extreme discounts for a *Black Friday* sale, the retailer may announce that only a specified number of these items are available per store, and that no rain checks will be given. This announcement puts customers on notice that supply is limited and if they are not at the store very early, they are unlikely to get the sale item. Manufacturers have an overbooking problem if they cannot meet promised delivery dates for the product, as does a contractor who cannot complete a project by its scheduled due date. Some businesses may quote aggressive delivery dates to get the order, but risk customer unhappiness or loss if the dates are not met. Some customers require that contracts provide for a financial penalty if due dates are missed.

In short, overbooking, in whatever form, can be a viable revenue management strategy, provided the cost of customer dissatisfaction is minimized.

## Bundling and Unbundling

Deciding whether to price a group of goods and services with a single package price, or to adopt *a la carte* pricing, is a critical decision in revenue management. The most visible example of this issue is the huge increase in add-on fees promulgated by most airlines in recent years. At one time, the ticket price included all services connected to the flight, with the exception of liquor on board for non-first-class passengers. Then airlines began to price separately a variety of elements of the flying experience, only some of which may be deemed optional choices by the passenger. The following are some of the separate charges that have emerged:

- Change of booking to an alternate flight
- On-board meals
- Checked luggage, and, for a few airlines, carry-on luggage
- Preferred seating (aisle, exit row, etc.)
- Early boarding
- A paper ticket rather than an electronic one
- Restroom access, proposed by at least one airline

Moreover, the addition of these fees was not a case of classic unbundling, where the price of the base service is reduced by pricing some elements separately. Rather, these fees have been add-ons, leaving ticket prices essentially unchanged (though airlines may claim that they permit the *continuation* of low fares). Indeed, industry reports suggest that these fees have added significantly to overall airline revenues. Although passengers actively dislike the practice of both the *nickel and diming* effect of numerous add-ons and the hassle of engaging in multiple transactions, overall passenger loads appear not to have suffered as a result, indicating a high degree of inelasticity for air travel. Some shifting of demand to carriers imposing fewer such fees, however, has been noted. Indeed, despite the negative reactions, the loss-of-business effect may be much less than that if equivalent fare increases were imposed. The apparent price at the time of first commitment may be a bigger factor than the vague knowledge that further fees lie ahead.

Initially, basic services such as luggage, meals, and itinerary changes were unbundled. More recently, added fees have focused on providing *value-added* extras, such as early boarding, more spacious seats, and preferred seating such as aisles and exit rows. Further, after unbundling so many services, some airlines have begun bundling their unbundled charges. American Airlines offered a package of one checked bag, early boarding, and no change fees for $68. Delta Airlines offered a limited-time $99 subscription of approximately three-month duration for one checked bag, early boarding, exit row seats, and extra frequent-flyer miles on all flights.

The bundling or unbundling decision is present in many lines of business. Examples include the following:

- For automobiles and consumer durable goods, some warranty coverage may be included as part of the product price, and some may be offered for sale separately as extended warranty coverage.
- Customers may buy a service contract for an appliance or buy service as needed.
- Vacationers may buy all-inclusive packages or buy each component (air, hotel, rental car, and perhaps meals) separately.

Some industries have moved away from unbundling. At one time, purchase of an automobile involved numerous choices of options; now most features are standard, and there are few options beyond color and upholstery. To some extent, availability of options has been replaced by expansion of the product line. Automobiles, computers and peripherals, and other big-ticket items have seen a proliferation of models. Rather than being able to customize a model, multiple precustomized models are offered.

## Free as a Price

As unlikely as it may sound, a price of zero is a valid revenue management technique, and one that is increasingly common. We take for granted all kinds of free information on the Internet, ranging from news to sports to recipes to medical information. We use free search engines to find all sorts of references in an instant. We interact via free e-mail and social media sites. Yet, somehow businesses are making money around all these free services. One author calls this outcome the *paradox of free*: "People are making lots of money charging nothing. Not nothing for everything, but nothing for enough that we have essentially created an economy as big as a good-sized country around the price of $0.00."[8]

The exceptionally low costs of electronic distribution underlie much of the free phenomenon, although the concept has been around for many years. When the creators of JELL-O® considered how to create demand for this new version of a somewhat-icky animal-processing by-product, they widely distributed free recipes to give people ideas on how to use it. Gillette used a near-free technique, selling its safety razors for very low prices and making its money on the subsequent sale of razor blades. This same technique is currently used by producers of video games, cellular telephones, and specialty coffee makers. Some printer and copier manufacturers offer very inexpensive printer–copier–fax machines. Once the customer purchases the machine, ongoing purchases of high-margin ink and toner cartridges are expected to follow. And, of course, radio and television broadcasts (in pre-cable days) were free to anyone who had the receiving equipment; third-party advertising paid the costs. These 20th-century examples of free were relatively few and far between. Twenty-first-century free is largely built around the economics of delivery via the Internet, where the component costs—processors, storage, and bandwidth—have been steadily decreasing, enabling the amount of free information to be steadily increasing.[9]

### Pseudo-Free

The word *free* is widely used to attract customers, but many uses are free in name only. *Buy one, get one free* is equivalent to a 50 percent price reduction; *free with purchase, free gift inside,* and *free shipping* all have their costs somehow incorporated into the price of the paid product. Free trials and free samples are truly free but have the expectation that paid purchases will follow from some percentage of the free recipients. These are not the modern meaning of a price of *free*.

### Variations of Free Price

Anderson points out that all types of *free* involve cross-subsidies of one kind or another: Paid products subsidize free products, paying customers subsidize free customers, or paying later subsidizes free now.[10] There are four variations of free goods and services.[11]

## Three-Party Markets

This arrangement is perhaps the oldest form of free, common in many media markets. Radio broadcasts have long been free to all, paid for by advertisers. This was also true of television broadcasts in pre-cable days. Even with cable, most broadcasts are still *free*, given that one has the now-more-complex receiving capability. Some newspapers and magazines are free, entirely supported by advertising, whereas others charge relatively nominal prices. To a great extent, online information and media content is free. In most cases, search engines that process, organize, and provide the extensive amount of online information are provided without a direct charge to the user.

## Direct Cross-Subsidy by the Provider

Something is provided free, in the hopes of gaining revenues from the customer in other ways. Banks provide free credit cards, making money from interest charges on carried balances, late and over-limit fees, and also from fees on merchants. Restaurants and bars offer free music or other entertainment to attract customers for food and drink purchases. Retailers offer a free item to induce customers to come into the store, where they may purchase other items. Entertainment providers may offer free admission to children, which will generate paid admissions by parents. Luxury automobile dealers offer free scheduled maintenance. Any seller who offers a range of products and services can offer something free to promote the sale of other offerings.

## Basic Version Free, Buy Upgrades

An expansion of the free-sample model, this version of free, sometimes called a *freemium*, offers a basic service, such as an e-mail account or a simple version of software, free to all users, while also offering upgraded versions for sale. The unusual economies of the computer or Internet world make for near-zero marginal costs; if a small percentage of users purchase upgrades, they profitably subsidize the many free users.

The freemium model has expanded into many areas. Skype provides free computer-to-computer calls, but charges for computer-to-phone calls. Many newspapers and magazines provide free web content, while charging for print content. Many *apps* for mobile phones, especially games, are free but one can buy game currency for a price.

The freemium model can be successful if one has a good-quality free product that customers want. This product needs wide distribution, as only a small percentage of the free users will buy the nonfree content. Digital distribution works best, as it keeps the cost of producing and distributing the free content to a minimum. Thus, the model is to generate wide use of the free product and profit from sales to a very small percentage of this large group.

## Other Nonmonetary Exchanges

We give away many things, such as used clothing, though many of these examples fall outside the business realm. Blogs offer free commentary from many sources, and Wikipedia has created a free encyclopedia from user inputs. This version of free is the least connected to revenue generation by other means.

The world of *free* has expanded, especially as electronic costs have declined substantially. This expansion enables *free* to be part of the revenue management toolkit of nearly all providers of goods and services.

## Customer Reward Programs

Many businesses offer customer reward programs as an inducement for continued patronage. Many customer reward programs are essentially deferred discounts; buying goods and services now earns benefits applicable to future purchases.

Perhaps the best known of the rewards programs are frequent-customer programs of the airlines and hotels. Customers earn points for each flight or hotel stay, redeemable for nearly free future flights or hotel stays and possibly for other merchandise as well. If indeed such programs really do induce continued patronage—a largely untested assumption—airlines and hotels are able to achieve the revenue benefits at relatively low cost. By managing and limiting the availability of frequent-flier seats, airlines attempt to minimize the displacement of a fare-paying passenger by a free rider. Hotels are usually less restrictive regarding customers' use of accumulated points. Further, many airlines sell frequent-flier miles to other businesses, such as hotels and car rental companies, thus generating some immediate cash flow from the program.

Credit card providers are another major user of rewards programs. Formats vary, from earning points redeemable for merchandise to points that may be exchanged for airline frequent-flier credit to cash rebate programs.

## Transaction Price Management

As noted earlier, the net revenue, or *pocket price*, from a sale is the critical number to the company. Net revenue may exceed the quoted price of the product or service as a result of additional fees and charges accompanying the transaction. The many fees charged by airlines above the stated ticket price, and the many fees charged by banks to holders of *free* checking accounts, are primary examples of managing the transaction price upward. Other common examples include shipping and handling fees imposed on many Internet or catalog sales, and automatic charges for future upgrades or supplements.

Perhaps more common are situations where the pocket price is below the quoted price. Such adjustments may include discounts for prompt payment, for the size of the current order, or for the annual volume of purchases. Various forms of rebates, incentives, or sales bonuses may be offered. Free shipping may be provided, and customer-specific allowances such as extended payment terms, cooperative advertising, or technical assistance may be given.[12] Each allowance or reduction reduces the pocket price, and the cumulative effect may be significant. Moreover, the authority to grant these various adjustments may be dispersed throughout the organization, and comprehensive reporting of net revenue typically does not occur. These features make the revenue management task more difficult.

In some cases, the net revenue from a given product or service may vary considerably among different customers. As a result, some customers are more expensive to service than others. This topic is explored further in Chapter 11.

# Conclusion

This chapter outlines some techniques that can be considered for companies seeking to manage their revenues. A variety of techniques are described that may accomplish the goal of increased revenues coupled with sustainable profit improvement. It is important to note though that successful revenue management requires not only knowledge of and attention to pricing on a broad scale but also familiarity with the net results at the individual customer or transaction level. If revenue management is not carefully and thoughtfully executed, considerable loss of revenue and profits can occur. Similarly, if a well-designed and well-researched technique is utilized that is congruent with the needs and interests of consumers and the market for the product, a substantial increase in revenues and sustainable profits may ensue. Careful consideration and research should precede the adoption of any revenue management strategy and technique, because mistakes can have costly outcomes.

# CHAPTER 6

# Customer Reactions to Revenue Management Techniques

Revenue management often involves variations in selling prices among customers or over time. The reaction of customers to these price variations may affect their future behavior. The research outlined in this chapter has shown that behavioral considerations, such as customers' perception of fairness and trust in their supplier, are of critical importance in developing long-term, profitable customers and optimal revenue management strategies. Customers who are satisfied with the current offered price, for example, are more likely to complete the transaction and are likely to consider dealing with the same seller in the future. Customers who are not satisfied with the current offered price may not complete the current transaction or may seek alternative future suppliers. Thus, revenue management involves not only economic considerations in setting prices but also behavioral considerations. How much additional revenue might be generated by a given technique is not the sole question; equally important is, how will current customers (and potential customers) react?

Revenue management is a long-term management activity. The response of customers to today's actions will impact, for better or worse, future revenues. Thus, customer reaction needs to be part of every revenue management analysis.

## Perceptions of Fairness

An interesting and critical factor when understanding consumer behavior is a customer's assessment of fairness. Kahneman, Knetsch, and Thaler introduce the notion of fairness into economic decision making.[1]

They observe many common actions that go beyond legal requirements, such as tipping service workers or maintaining a lost-and-found department. Presumably, these behaviors occur because they are perceived as fair, or at least customary, means of acting. Standard economic analysis, however, often focuses on profit-maximizing behavior without regard to behavioral characteristics of either buyers or sellers. These authors emphasize *fairness*, described as not exploiting all legal opportunities for gain.[2] Fairness has implications for revenue management decisions. If certain products are in very high demand due to a natural disaster—snow shovels, bottled water, batteries—should prices be substantially increased to profit from the temporarily high demand? Many would conclude that raising prices in those circumstances would be unfair and exploitative, especially given that the seller's costs did not increase.

Kahneman et al.[3] cite several examples where perceptions of fairness enter into pricing. In one example, an upcoming sporting event has unusually high demand and a limited number of tickets are available. Among three methods of distribution, a survey rated the first-come, first-served method as most fair (68 percent), a lottery as second (28 percent), and an auction (selling to highest bidder) as the least fair (4 percent). The auction, however, would probably maximize the seller's revenues.[4] In another example, a pair of scenarios was given:

1. A small house is rented to a fixed-income tenant but the owner's costs have increased substantially. Should the rent be increased, even though the tenant will be forced to move because the new amount is unaffordable?
2. An employee of a small business earns $15 an hour. Due to the closure of a large nearby plant, equally skilled and reliable workers could now be hired for $12 per hour. Should the pay of the current employee be reduced?

Respondents to these scenarios found the rent increase to be completely fair (39 percent) or at least acceptable (36 percent), but found the pay reduction to be very unfair (49 percent) or somewhat unfair (34 percent).[5] Price increases based on higher costs were deemed fair, but a pay cut due to a greater labor pool from high unemployment was not.

Perceptions of fairness occur not only on the part of the customer but on the part of the seller as well. A common psychology experiment, reported by numerous authors, involves giving a sum of money (say $20) to person A, which is to be shared with anonymous person B. Person A may establish any split desired, and person B then has the right to accept or reject. If B accepts, the money is divided as proposed by A; if B rejects the split, neither party gets anything. Pure economics (self-interest) might suggest that A should keep most of the money, allocating only a small amount to B, and that B is better off getting something rather than nothing. Repeated experiments found that the A players frequently offered nearly equal splits (usually about 60 percent for A and 40 percent for B), and that B players frequently rejected very unbalanced splits, even though they got nothing as a result. Thus, both sides brought a sense of fairness to the transaction.[6]

## Fairness in Pricing

There are many dimensions to what customers perceive as *fair* in pricing, some of which may seem to defy economic rationality. Understanding these customer perceptions is helpful in establishing revenue management strategies.

Surcharges, for example, are usually less well received than discounts. A surcharge for paying by a credit card would be perceived negatively where a discount for paying cash would not. A differential could be justified on the grounds that a seller incurs fees on credit card transactions, but customers do not accept that as justification for a surcharge. Presenting the differential as a penalty (surcharge) for using a credit card rather than as a reward (discount) for not doing so adversely impacts the perception.[7]

Coca-Cola once floated the idea of creating vending machines that could adjust the price charged for a cold drink in response to the outdoor temperature, on the grounds that higher demand for a cold drink on a hot day justified a higher price.[8] The idea was widely criticized as extremely unfair and was quickly disavowed.

My wife and I once took a cruise in response to a *two-for-one* promotion by the cruise line. During the course of the cruise, we often interacted with a couple from Seattle. At some point, we commented that we were motivated to take the cruise—our first—by the two-for-one pricing. Our Seattle friend was upset by this information. He had signed up for the cruise at about the same time, and had specifically asked his travel agent if any special deals were available; moreover, he was a repeat customer of the cruise line. Although he was satisfied with his full-price fare when he signed up for the cruise, he became dissatisfied upon learning that some-one else had gotten a much better deal, and was annoyed for the remain-der of the cruise. What seemed fair at the time changed to a perception of unfairness once he learned what another customer had paid.[9]

Thus, fairness is often perceived in comparison to what is called a *reference price*.[10] Reference prices may take various forms: posted or list prices, past prices, current competitor prices, expected prices based on advertisements, and so forth. The reference price is what the customer *expects to pay*. Reductions from the reference price are generally well received, whereas amounts in excess of the reference price are generally not. In the forgoing examples, the surcharge for credit card use and the higher price for a cold drink on a hot day were perceived as exceeding the reference, or usual, price. In the cruise example, the customer's reference price changed upon learning what others had been charged.

## Trust and Revenue Management Decisions

In addition to fairness, trust is also a dimension of consumer behavior that should be considered when devising and applying revenue manage-ment approaches.

### Relationship Marketing

The concept of relationship marketing has emerged to signify a strategy for managing and nurturing a company's interactions with actual and potential customers, with the hope that an ongoing buyer–seller rela-tionship will ensue. When customers develop a trusting relationship with their suppliers, a positive outcome is likely for the seller. For example, a buyer may perceive that transaction costs and risk are lower in deal-ing with the same seller over time. This perception results in a sense of trust that the supplier is considering the best interests of the customer. McMahon-Beattie, Yeoman, Palmer, and Mudie raise the question of whether the variable pricing inherent in revenue management is consistent with developing trust between buyer and seller. If a seller is offering lower prices to certain buyers, such as new customers, how should a loyal customer respond? Believing that a seller operates in this manner or observing an increasingly complex pricing structure (a frequent result of revenue management) may erode the trust that a buyer has in a supplier. The authors make four recommendations to practitioners of revenue management with regard to trust.[11]

1. Ask if the benefits of flexible pricing outweigh the operational costs and possible reduction of customer trust.
2. Make sure that the bases for flexible pricing are made known.
3. Offer customers ways they can save money by qualifying for lower prices.
4. Do not punish regular, loyal customers by charging them higher prices without providing them some benefit for their loyalty.

Customer trust is important; revenue management techniques can coexist with customer trust, but careful management is needed to ensure that trust is not lost, since there may be significant adverse consequences when this occurs.

## Presentation of Prices

How prices are presented to customers has a bearing on customer reaction and behavior. The tendency to use 99 pricing is well known. A price of $3.99 is viewed differently from a price of $4.00, whereas lowering a $3.99 price to $3.91 would probably have little effect. The belief is that buyers focus on the lead digit(s) in the price. This phenomenon applies to high-price items as well; a new car is likely to be advertised at $23,999 rather than $24,000.

As mentioned earlier, presenting a price as a discount or reduction from a normal (reference) price is better received than a surcharge. We observe, however, several exceptions to this norm. Airlines, which compete on the basis of the posted fare, have in recent years imposed numerous surcharges or extra fees. Fees have been charged for checked baggage, overweight baggage, early boarding, preferred seating, food, pillows and blankets, and other items. Even though customers profess considerable annoyance at all these fees, there is little evidence that they would prefer a higher stated fare and fewer, if any, extra charges. Banks also compete on the basis of free or low-priced services—free checking, no-annual-fee credit cards, and the like. They too have an array of fees—for late payment, overdrafts, exceeding the credit limit, failure to maintain a minimum balance, and the like. In the airline case, most customers will incur some fees, particularly for checked baggage. In the bank case, however, nearly all fees are avoidable by careful management of one's accounts.

Rewards and penalties in pricing operate much the same as discounts and surcharges. When rewards are offered for ongoing patronage—as is common with airlines and hotels—they usually take the form of future benefits rather than current price reductions. Customers pay the same current price as others, but earn credits toward free or reduced-price flights or rooms, or other benefits. It is considered acceptable to offer frequent flier credits, but it would not be well received for an airline to charge a new flier a higher fare. Grocery stores, on the other hand, often have *loyalty card* programs. Cardholders receive a discounted price but noncardholders do not. However, anyone can get a card simply by applying; prior patronage is not required. The *loyalty* in a loyalty card program is relatively meaningless, as all cardholders are treated equally.

Health clubs were once known for charging high initial fees for an annual membership. Their revenue model was to sign up as many new customers as possible, recognizing that usage would tend to drop off after a few months of initial enthusiasm, and many memberships would not be renewed. Many clubs following this model tended not to survive very long, as the supply of new customers dwindled. More recently, a new model emerged: modest signup fees (often under $50) and low monthly fees (often under $20). The monthly fee is automatically charged to the customer's credit card, and the customer may cancel at any time. This approach appears to be a more successful revenue model, as the initial commitment is much less, and there is no major renewal decision. Even though usage may continue to be sporadic after the period of initial enthusiasm, inertia and the low monthly fee cause many customers to passively maintain the membership.

In some cases, the best means for presenting price is not clear. Consider a bank offering home equity loans. It could quote its annual percentage rate for the loan, or the monthly payment. Assume that competitors are offering a 6 percent rate, and a particular bank decides to promote a 5.25 percent rate. On a five-year, $25,000 loan, the monthly payment would fall by only 1.6 percent, from $483.32 to $474.65, while the quoted rate fell by 12.5 percent. The rate would be a more appealing price to advertise, although the monthly payment may be more relevant to the customer's decision.

### Expectations of Price

Customers base their reference prices in part on past behavior. Businesses that seem to always have a *sale*—auto dealers, furniture and appliance stores, and the clothing department of many department stores—may condition their customers to always expect a sale, and to defer their purchases until a sale occurs. Stores that follow a consistent *everyday-low-price* approach are much less subject to this behavior. Sears once observed that most of their appliance business occurred during sales. They tried to convert to an everyday low price approach but were not successful in doing so. Customers continued to believe that a sale was coming soon and deferred purchases in anticipation. Sears soon reverted to its former system, validating customer expectations. In 2011, automakers adopted a *fresh marketing strategy* for 2011 models: lower sticker prices.[12] There is little evidence that this worked; the industry continues to rely heavily on rebates and low-cost financing in selling cars. Customer expectations concerning the firm's pricing behavior are important, and once established, they are not easily changed.

### Acceptable Price Discrimination

The earlier examples—credit card surcharges, higher soft drink pricing on hot days, and cruise pricing—were cases in which pricing differences were generally deemed inappropriate. There are, however, many forms of price discrimination that are considered generally acceptable. Perhaps the most common one is the senior citizen discount (which I have come to appreciate), though there is little economic justification for this differential, nor is it evident that it enhances revenue. A senior discount for the same product or service offered to others is distinct from a restaurant's senior menu, for example, which offers smaller servings that are perhaps better suited to a senior's smaller appetite. Discounts for goods or services sold to members of an organization are also widely accepted. Many businesses offer discounts to AAA or AARP members.

Public colleges and universities charge lower tuition fees for in-state students than for out-of-state students. This differential is justified on the grounds that in-state students, or their families, also support the institution through their state taxes. In many cases, the tuition differential may not be great enough; some state taxpayer subsidy of out-of-state students still occurs.

Children often are charged lower prices for meals, transportation, and admissions to entertainment events than adults. This difference is in part justified in that children may consume fewer goods and services. It likely enhances revenue in that it encourages families to patronize the business, which they may not do if every member had to pay full price.

Bars sometimes offer *ladies' night* where females get drinks at reduced prices. Although gender discrimination is usually frowned upon, this promotion is often considered benign and revenue positive, in that (a) many females are not heavy drinkers and (b) the likely presence of (especially unattached) females is likely to considerably enhance male patronage.

## Dimensions of Fairness in Pricing

Differential pricing is based on many characteristics, but there are some general principles of fairness, as suggested by Phillips.[13]

- Price differences that are product or service based are more acceptable than differences that are customer based. We do, however, observe numerous instances of customer-based price differentials.

- Discounts, promotions, and rewards are better received than surcharges or penalties. Although this behavior is common, we do observe some cases where fees and surcharges are used.
- Availability of the price to the individual. Lower prices based on factors such as advance booking or timing of the service are conceivably available to anyone, whereas lower prices based on age (child or senior discounts) are not. If customers could have taken advantage of the lower price but chose not to meet the conditions, they are more likely to think it fair than if it was not available to them at all.
- Simple, open, easy-to-understand pricing is preferred to complex, unusual, and hidden price structures. Lawyers, for example, often charge a rate per hour; although the structure is simple, the process for timekeeping may not be well understood. Similarly, pricing of medical services is often perceived as complex and hidden.

An additional dimension of fairness, especially with regard to price *changes*, is known as the *principle of dual entitlement*.[14] Buyers are entitled to a *reasonable* price, and sellers are entitled to a *reasonable* profit. Although luxury goods—artwork, jewelry, sports cars, and the like—may carry very high prices, items that are closer to necessities should be priced *fairly*. Raising prices in response to cost increases is fair, but raising prices in times of supply shortage or temporarily high demand, such as a storm, is not.

Bolton, Warlop, and Alba conducted several experiments on consumer perceptions of the fairness or unfairness of pricing.[15] They concluded that a general lack of consumer knowledge of prices, costs, and profits led to perceptions that prices, or price changes, were unfair. Consumers tended to regularly underestimate the price effects of inflation over time. They attribute price differentials between store types—such as full-service department stores versus discount stores—to profit differences rather than cost differences. They also tended to underestimate the levels of costs beyond those of the product itself—the overhead, selling, administrative, and other costs of doing business. Finally, they tended to substantially overestimate profit margins, often attributing profit percentages in the

20 to 30 percent range, even for retailers such as grocery stores, which in fact typically earn low-single-digit profit margins. As a result, consumers usually feel that prices should be considerably lower than they are. The consistent underestimation of costs and overestimation of profitability poses a major problem to revenue management, as customers tend to feel that most prices are too high.

## Research on Fairness of Revenue Management

Many authors have studied the reaction of customers to the variable pricing techniques commonly employed in revenue management. Kimes and Wirtz examined this question in the golf industry.[16] Arrival time controls in the form of requiring tee time reservations and charging for no-shows were deemed fair, as was time-of-day pricing. Basing the price on when the reservation was booked (higher fees for bookings longer in advance) was viewed negatively, as was varying price according to short-term demand fluctuations. When variable prices were invoked, discounts were viewed more positively than surcharges.

Shoemaker studied the relationship of customer loyalty to pricing practices in the hotel industry.[17] The importance of loyalty varies from industry to industry. For airlines, customer choice may be limited since only one or two airlines may service the route the customer desires, making loyalty to a particular airline a minor factor in the purchase. There are typically many hotels serving a customer's destination, however, and thus, loyalty to a particular brand may be a much more important factor in the choice. Charging a higher-than-normal rate for a high-demand time might alienate the loyal customer, causing them to switch both current and future business to a competitor. Many hotels use loyalty-card systems to help identify regular customers. If this information is entered early in the reservation process, pricing could be adjusted to reflect the customer's history and frequency of patronage.

Shoemaker also reports on an experiment in framing.[18] Customers booking a hotel room in Las Vegas were presented with one of two options. Option A offered a room for $159, with a $30 upgrade providing a room on a high floor with a good view of the Las Vegas Strip; Option B offered the high floor room with the view for $189, or a room anywhere else in the hotel for $30 less. Thus, one option involved a surcharge for a *better* room, while the other offered a discount for forgoing the view. Consistent with the notion that discounts are better received than surcharges, the hotel found that only 13.6 percent of those offered Option A chose to upgrade to the higher priced room, but 20.6 percent of those offered Option B opted for the higher priced room. Quoting the higher price with the possibility of a discount generated about $30,000 per month more in room revenue than quoting a lower price with the extra cost upgrade. Option B was perceived as the hotel looking out for the guest's best interests by offering the best room with the opportunity to downgrade and save money.

## Summary

This chapter has highlighted the importance of behavioral considerations when developing revenue management strategies. Research demonstrates the importance of considering the impact of revenue management approaches on a customers' perception of fairness and their trust in the supplier. These behavioral considerations are important to developing long-term profitable customers.

# CHAPTER 7

# Additional Tools for Analysis of Revenue Management Decisions

In this chapter, we first revisit the topic of contribution margin analysis. A classic case is used to illustrate the limitations of this methodology. We then consider the economic tool of analysis of price elasticity. Finally, we discuss willingness to pay as a factor in the analysis of revenue management decisions.

## The Special Order Problem

Special order problems are used in managerial accounting as a common illustration of the application of contribution margin analysis for revenue management decisions. The problem is characterized as an opportunity for additional business coupled with a reduction from usual prices. This is a common format for many revenue management decisions: Will a price reduction bring additional revenues and additional profits? Special order problems typically assume that the special order is somehow separate from the company's normal business, and that accepting the reduced price will not have an adverse impact on pricing for other customers. But that assumption should be viewed with considerable caution.

The *Baldwin Bicycle Company* case is a classic instructional case in special order pricing.[1] Based on a real company's situation, it takes place in a historical time frame where big discount stores are just emerging on the retail scene. Baldwin, a bicycle manufacturer, currently sells its product through sporting goods stores, bicycle shops, and other local retailers. Baldwin now has an opportunity to contract for a large volume of private-label bicycles for a national discount chain, at a price well below its normal selling price. An initial contribution margin analysis shows this opportunity to be very profitable. Even though the order is large, the existence of adequate excess capacity removes the need for investment in additional production resources. Some additional working capital investment is required, in the form of additional inventories and accounts receivable. Baldwin estimates that sales to its regular customers may decline by 3 percent, but the contribution margin analysis remains very positive. When the case is analyzed further, however, one concludes that the long-term outlook for Baldwin is dismal.

Initially, the special pricing appears to apply to 20 percent of Baldwin's sales. But several events will likely occur as time passes:

- Retail customers will purchase more and more bicycles through discount stores, gradually eroding Baldwin's normal business base.
- Baldwin's regular customers will press for price reductions to remain competitive.
- Baldwin's practice of selling to different customers at different prices is likely to create customer ill will.
- The discount chain will likely seek further price reductions in the future.

As Baldwin sells more and more product at reduced prices, it will be increasingly unable to operate at an overall profit.

The analysis also suggests that Baldwin's decline will occur whether or not it accepts the special order. If Baldwin does not produce the private-label bicycles for the discount store, another manufacturer surely will. Either way, Baldwin's current situation cannot be sustained.

### The Lesson of Baldwin Bicycle

Although special pricing, in whatever context, may initially contribute incrementally to profits, keep the long-term picture in mind. Where will this special pricing lead? It may signify a fundamental change in the industry, as in the Baldwin Bicycle case, where retail distribution was about to undergo a major structural transformation. Even though initially limited, the special (lower) pricing may gradually become the pricing norm, as with low airline fares and automobile rebates. In either case, a simple contribution margin analysis does not suffice. The lesson states that revenue management techniques in themselves are not harmful, but inadequate analysis of their long-term effects can be devastating.

## Beyond Contribution Margin

Contribution margin analysis is relevant for revenue management applications that are limited in scope, apply to a small subset of sales, and will not erode significant sales at normal prices. Where these assumptions do not hold, analysis of a revenue management application becomes more complex.

A panel discussion at the 1989 annual meeting of the American Accounting Association featured some of the leading scholars in management accounting commenting on the pros and cons of contribution margin as a metric for short-term pricing decisions.[2] The following are some of the highlights of that discussion:

- Companies don't get rich using a contribution margin approach. John Shank cited what he called Shank's axiom: *If the problem is small enough so that contribution margin analysis is relevant then it can't have a very big impact on a company. And if the possible impact in a decision setting is major, if it can really affect a company in a major way, then it's silly to consider most of the factors to be fixed.*[3]
- Shank could identify no major successes from contribution margin analysis in the real world, but could find many failures, in industries such as airlines, steel, and paper.[4]
- Robert Kaplan, a major advocate of activity-based costing—a full-cost rather than contribution approach—pointed out that fixed costs keep growing within the cost structures of virtually all companies. Although he acknowledged that contribution margin analysis is valid for short-term optimization, he emphasized that there is also a role for full-cost information. Contribution margin works well in relatively simple

situations, but most companies have extensive product lines and complex product interactions. Full cost data—especially if it is activity based—helps identify which products are currently profitable and which are not. Contribution analysis may then help make incremental improvements to products that need them.[5]

- Kaplan acknowledged the positive results from a special order price that exceeds variable cost. The danger, he felt, is that more and more of these special-pricing opportunities will present themselves. As this type of pricing grows, the conclusion that fixed costs are not affected becomes less and less valid.[6]

These views support the cautions expressed earlier. Some of the major examples of a contribution-pricing form of revenue management—airlines, automotive companies, and others—have not been successful from a profit viewpoint. Contribution analysis is relevant for short-term optimization only. Initially, revenue management (in the form of pricing just above marginal cost) did help to fill unused capacity on short notice or combat a competitor. Once marginal cost became the basis for widespread pricing, failing to consider fixed costs became a serious problem. The message? Use contribution analysis sparingly!

A more thorough and comprehensive analysis goes beyond basic contribution margin analysis. The following questions might be considered in analyzing discounts or other price concessions:[7]

- What is the current profitability of the business? If currently unprofitable, can price concessions generate enough volume increase to make the business profitable, despite the lower contribution margin? If currently profitable, would price concessions gain new customers or increase volume with current customers?
- If new customers are attracted by price concessions, will they continue to patronize the business?
- If price concessions are offered only to new customers, how will existing customers react?

- If price concessions do substantially increase volume, can the company provide adequate service for the increased demand?
- If price concessions are given frequently, will customers keep expecting lower prices always?
- If competitors match price concessions and lower prices become the industry norm, can the business continue to be profitable?

## Revenue Drivers

The term *cost drivers* has become a standard element of cost management; similarly, the concept of *revenue drivers* indicates variables that influence revenues. Perhaps, the most common customer-based revenue driver is customer satisfaction. Many businesses employ follow-up telephone calls, comment cards, and surveys to gain input from customers on their satisfaction with a recent service encounter or product purchase. Among the questions commonly included, each with a range of choices, are *would you patronize us again?* and *would you recommend us to others?* Do these surveys work? One study for a large hotel chain found a statistically significant relationship between customer satisfaction and future financial performance.[8]

Perhaps the most extensive work on revenue drivers has been done by Shields and Shields.[9] They identified 25 revenue drivers implicit in existing management concepts, such as activity-based costing, the balanced scorecard, and strategic cost analysis. Many characteristics can drive revenues. Some are marketing-type measures such as brand image, price, market share, and customer satisfaction. Others are internal, production-based characteristics, such as capacity, quality, employee skill, economies of scale, and the development of new products and services. External forces such as the extent of competition also impact revenues, though often in a negative fashion.

## Elasticity of Demand

Elasticity of demand is another consideration to be evaluated in applying revenue management. Elasticity of demand with respect to price—commonly called simply *price elasticity* or *price elasticity of demand*—is a measure of the expected change in demand in response to a change in price. Attributed to 19th-century economist Alfred Marshall,[10] price elasticity measures the percentage change in quantity demanded (Q) relative to (divided by) the percentage change in price (P).

$$\text{Price elasticity} = (\Delta Q/Q)/(\Delta P/P)$$

where $\Delta$ signifies the amount of change. Price elasticity is typically negative, following the usual economic assumption that demand falls as price rises and vice versa.

Revenue equals price times quantity of items sold. Increasing the price will increase revenue in the absence of a quantity change, but increasing price usually decreases the quantity sold. Similarly, decreasing the price will decrease revenue in the absence of a quantity change, but decreasing price usually increases the quantity sold. The net outcome of a price change can be estimated if we have an idea of the price elasticity of that product. Price elasticity outcomes fall into one of five categories:

1. A price is *perfectly inelastic* (elasticity = 0) if a price change will have no effect on quantity demanded in either direction. Thus, a price increase will increase revenue and a price decrease will decrease revenue. It is unlikely that goods with perfectly price-inelastic demand exist at all, except in a narrow range or a narrow time period.
2. A price is *relatively inelastic* (elasticity < 0 but > -1) if a price change will result in a proportionately smaller change in quantity demanded. Thus, a price increase will still increase revenue even though the quantity sold decreases somewhat, and a price decrease will decrease revenue, even though the quantity sold increases somewhat. For example, suppose 10,000 units are currently sold at $10 each, generating revenue of $100,000. If price elasticity is -0.5, a 10 percent price increase would reduce demand by 5 percent; 9,500 units would now be sold at $11, increasing revenue to $104,500. Similarly, a 10 percent price reduction would increase demand by 5 percent; 10,500 units would now be sold at $9, decreasing revenue to $94,500.

3. A price is *unit elastic* (elasticity = –1) if a price change results in a proportionately equal change in quantity demanded. The net effect of a price change on revenue should be zero. In practice, a small change would be calculated. Again consider the situation where 10,000 units are currently sold at $10 each, generating revenue of $100,000. A 10 percent price increase to $11 and a 10 percent quantity decrease to 9,000 would yield revenue of $99,000, as would a 10 percent price decrease to $9 and a 10 percent quantity increase to 11,000 units. Although an exact elasticity of –1 is relatively unlikely, what is important is that one is the dividing line between price changes affecting revenue in the *same* direction (as in Category 2) and price changes affecting revenue in the *opposite* direction (as in Category 4, next).

4. A price is *relatively elastic* (elasticity < –1) if a price change results in a proportionately greater change in quantity demanded. Thus, a price increase will cause a large enough decrease in quantity sold so that total revenue falls, and a price decrease will cause a large enough increase in quantity sold so that total revenue increases. Again suppose 10,000 units are currently sold at $10 each, generating revenue of $100,000. If the price elasticity is –1.3, then a 10 percent price increase would reduce demand by 13 percent; 8,700 units would now be sold at $11, decreasing revenue to $95,700. Similarly, a 10 percent price reduction would increase demand by 13 percent; 11,300 units would now be sold at $9, increasing revenue to $101,700.

5. In the extreme case, a price is *perfectly elastic* (elasticity is infinite) if a price increase would cause demand to drop to zero, and a price decrease would cause demand to explode to infinity. Such situations have not been found to exist.

Thus, the critical question is whether one faces a *relatively inelastic* or *relatively elastic* demand. If a company faces a relatively inelastic demand, there is little motivation for price decreases, but price increases may be desirable. If a company faces a relatively elastic demand, then price reductions can lead to greater revenues. Managers must have an understanding of the price elasticity of their products or services in making revenue management decisions.

### Is Elasticity Always Negative?

The previous discussion implies that the measure of price elasticity of demand starts at zero and declines from there. There are two extremely limited circumstances, each named after the economist who described the phenomenon, where a positive elasticity exists and quantity demanded *rises* as the price rises.

A so-called *Veblen good* is one where a high price signifies status and exclusivity. A Rolls-Royce automobile or a Rolex watch sells for a very high price. Customers may buy that brand at ever-higher prices, not because it offers superior services, but because it signifies wealth and prestige. A so-called *Giffen good* is one that fills a need, but is inferior to other goods. For example, suppose rice is a basic food and it is the cheapest form of nutrition and hunger satisfaction. Consumers, even the poorest, normally seek to buy a variety of foods—rice, meat, vegetables, and so forth. If the price of rice rises, but remains less than those of alternative foods, the result may be that consumers buy *more* rice. Their limited food budget is increasingly used to purchase this lowest cost form of nutrition, necessitating reductions in the purchase of meat and other superior foods. Both of these situations have very limited applicability. For the analysis of revenue management decisions, price elasticity of demand can be assumed to be negative.

### Price Elasticity of Supply

Parallel to the customer response to price changes is the producer's response. Price elasticity of supply has a parallel definition, namely the percentage change in quantity supplied relative to (divided by) the percentage change in price. Demand elasticity is typically negative, whereas supply elasticity is almost always positive. That is, producers will supply more at higher prices than at lower prices.

Among the factors impacting a producer's ability to respond to increased demand are the availability of capacity (physical, personnel, and materials); the presence of inventories; and the complexity and lead times involved in production.[11] For example, an increased demand for agricultural products is affected by the timing and length of the growing season. Although customers generally prefer to purchase greater quantities when prices are lower, producers may be unwilling to produce these greater quantities (or perhaps any quantity at all) at lower prices. If production is not profitable at lower prices, producers will generally not produce that item, at least in the long run. This duality of price elasticity of demand and price elasticity of supply maintains a degree of overall balance in the system.

### Applying Elasticity to Revenue Management

Keep in mind that price elasticity is an economic construct. Although it exists, it is not easily measurable. A company may experiment with a reduced (sale) price for a limited time period. Although it observes an increase in demand while the sale is on, it is not clear that the higher demand will be sustained if the reduced price continues indefinitely. It is possible that offering the sale price merely changed the timing of demand, causing some customers to buy while the sale was on, rather than later. Further, price elasticity may change over time, and may be influenced by one company's prices relative to its competitors. Also, the elasticity may be different at different price levels along the demand curve. A 10 percent change in the price of gasoline may have a different demand effect when gasoline sells for $4.00 per gallon than when it sells at $1.75 per gallon.

In thinking about price elasticity, consider the big picture as well as the firm-specific picture. Suppose the demand for product A is a *derived demand*, dependent on the demand for product B into which it is incorporated. The demand for product A is typically not elastic overall, as price changes for product A are not likely to result in changes in the sales of product B. For example, a decrease in the price of tires sold to auto manufacturers probably will not change the demand for new cars. A price decrease by a supplier of tires may appear elastic, but auto makers are likely merely switching their purchases from other suppliers. If competitors match the price decrease, the apparent elasticity largely disappears. The elasticity concept is thus more difficult to apply on business-to-business sales, many of which represent derived demand for downstream products. Elasticity is most useful for products sold to end users (consumers), where price reduction may result in an increase in overall demand.

Because elasticity depends on many factors, such as the current price level, the time frame of the price change, and the number of sellers making a price change, numerical calculation can be difficult and may not be particularly useful. Rather, we seek to use the concept more generally, to understand the sensitivity of demand to changing prices.[12]

Although price elasticity of demand is not easily measured, some of the factors that contribute to it include the following:[13]

- How necessary is the product? Essential products tend to have lower elasticity.
- How big an expense item is it for the consumer? Buyers may be more price sensitive on expensive items than on low-cost items.
- Consumable goods may be less price sensitive in the short term because buyers have limited opportunities to adjust. An increase in the price of gasoline may lead drivers to reduce travel in the short term, but to buy a car with better gas mileage in the long term. On the other hand, durable goods may be more price sensitive in the short term, as the buyer may be able to put off purchasing until prices are more favorable.
- Are good substitutes available, such as a substantially identical product from another supplier or a similar product that fulfills the same function? If substitutes are available, elasticity is likely to be greater. However, a high degree of brand loyalty or supplier loyalty would lead to less elasticity.
- How long might the price change be in effect? If a price increase is expected to be of short duration, consumers may be able to defer purchasing (or accelerate purchases and build inventories in the face of a short-term price decrease).
- Have all sellers changed their price? If not, short-term reaction may be limited, as consumers continue to buy from their usual supplier. In the longer term, consumers may seek a new supplier. If all sellers have changed prices, consumers may search for substitutes, or forgo the product entirely. As airlines increase fares via add-on fees, and as the intangible costs of flying increase due to fewer flights, increased security, and

other hassles, some passengers will forgo travel, and others will switch to substitutes, such as auto or train travel, or to more indirect substitutes such as virtual business meetings rather than face-to-face meetings.

• Who pays the bill? Health care has been largely price inelastic, in part because it has a high degree of necessity and also because the payer is often a third party, not the consumer.

Understanding something about customer response to price changes, whether upward or downward, is helpful to the effective use of revenue management.

## Willingness to Pay

Somewhat related to the concept of price elasticity is the concept of willingness to pay, sometimes referred to as the customer's *reservation price*.[14] For most goods and services, it is assumed that there is a maximum price that a customer will pay. This reservation price likely varies from customer to customer; so a single determination of willingness to pay is impossible.

In revenue management decisions, the motive for a price reduction is usually to increase revenue by bringing in new customers who are unwilling to buy at existing prices. Thus, the goal is to price below the reservation price for an additional group of customers. Another goal is to accomplish attracting new customers without reducing the price to existing customers. Early applications of revenue management by airlines sought to increase purchases by leisure travelers while maintaining the current purchases by business travelers. Techniques such as advance purchase requirements and minimum stay requirements were enacted to try to *build a fence* around the reduced price offerings that would exclude most business travelers.

The economic concept of *consumer surplus* is defined as willingness to pay minus the price actually paid. Again, consumer surplus varies from customer to customer, given that willingness to pay varies. The larger the consumer surplus, the happier the customer. But a large consumer surplus also means that the seller has *left money on the table* by not extracting a price closer to the buyer's willingness to pay. To the extent that revenue management features different prices for different customers, sellers try to capture as much of the variable consumer surplus as possible but at the risk of customer dissatisfaction. This issue was discussed further in the preceding chapter on customer response.

## Conclusion

Contribution margin analysis is a commonly used technique for evaluation of revenue management decisions, but it must be used with caution. Contribution margin analysis is most appropriate for small, short-term changes. When revenue management decisions may have broader, longer-term effects, further analysis is needed.

Economic concepts of price elasticity provide a useful way of thinking about the demand effects of price changes. Although elasticity may be hard to measure, it is useful to consider how both customers and competitors will react to a pricing decision.

# CHAPTER 8

# Revenue Management and Capacity Analysis

Two topics with special relevance for revenue management are *capacity analysis*, especially the capacity model developed by Computer Aided Manufacturing-International (CAM-I), and the *theory of constraints* (TOC), as set forth by Eli Goldratt in *The Goal* and subsequent publications. This chapter discusses capacity analysis; the TOC is presented in Chapter 9.

Considerations of capacity are central to revenue management, which is about generating additional revenue (selling unused capacity) in a profitable way.

## Background: Capacity Management

Concern regarding the analysis, costing, and management of capacity has been a long-standing issue in accounting, finance, and management. McNair and Vangermeersch provide a historical summary of 12 major capacity management concepts, ranging from the early 20th-century work of Henry Gantt to the theories and techniques of the late 20th century.[1] One pervasive issue involves how to address the cost of capacity not currently utilized in production: Should the cost be identified separately or should the cost be incorporated into product costs and borne by current production, even though the excess capacity does not contribute to current production? This issue has been discussed for the better part of a century, and will not be addressed here.

Another prevalent theme focuses on management techniques for the efficient use of capacity. Since about 1980, several capacity-related management techniques have emerged on the scene.[2] Material requirement planning (MRP) focuses on coordinating material acquisition, production scheduling, and process control for more efficient use of manufacturing capacity. Just-in-time (JIT) production tends to focus on small-cell man-ufacturing, with techniques designed to minimize waiting, material or product movement, and inventories. The TOC emphasizes the identifi-cation and management of bottlenecks (constraints) in the production process. The capacity utilization bottleneck efficiency system (CUBES) extended TOC by developing an 11-factor model of capacity utilization. Finally, the CAM-I model emphasized the strategic use of capacity. Read-ers interested in further details on these topics are encouraged to consult McNair and Vangermeersch.[3]

McNair and Vangermeersch consider capacity management at three levels.[4] At the operational or short-term level, they summarize seven relevant practices, none of which involve revenue issues. At the tactical or intermediate-term level, they cite 12 common elements of the various capacity management models; again, none mentions revenue. Only at the strategic or long-term level do revenue issues seem to enter the picture. Four of their seven core features mention value creation, market strategy, and customer and market requirements. Indeed, they state that, from a long-term perspective, "capacity is redefined as the value-creating capa-bility of the firm and is tied only loosely to the underlying costs and resources that create this value."[5]

Despite the extensive capacity literature over a long time period, the predominant themes remain regarding how to deal with the cost of unuti-lized capacity and how to utilize capacity in the most production-efficient way. Both themes have limited connection to revenue management. However, two of the previously cited techniques do have relevance to rev-enue management. The CAM-I model, discussed in this chapter, takes a strategic look at capacity utilization, including the question of how much is truly revenue producing. This analysis serves as a foundation for consid-ering how to generate additional revenues from one's capacity by chang-ing strategies or policies. The TOC model, discussed in the next chapter, explicitly incorporates throughput (net revenue) as the leading metric for making capacity decisions.

## Capacity Analysis

As mentioned earlier, revenue management is about generating additional revenue by selling unused capacity in a profitable way. Thus, it is essential to know what one's capacity is, and how it is currently deployed. In the early applications of revenue management, relevant capacity was obvious: the number of seats on a flight, the number of rooms in a hotel, the number of autos at a rental agency, and so forth. But as revenue management expanded to more sophisticated levels, a better analysis and understanding of capacity was needed.

Much of the traditional capacity literature is concerned with overhead costing: how to spread the cost of capacity, including unused capacity, to products. Such considerations have little to no value from a revenue management perspective, since mere allocations of cost do nothing to generate revenues or influence real profits. Indeed, such allocations can prove harmful to revenue management if the allocated costs adversely influence price setting.

CAM-I—a group made up of large industrial companies, consultants, and others—developed a useful model showing how capacity is used.[6] Their model begins by analyzing how capacity is currently being used. The four main components of capacity are physical, personnel, processes, and supply:

- Physical capacity—buildings, equipment, and technology—is generally available 24/7.
- Personnel capacity is present to the extent management decides to provide it. Workers can be taken off the job and sent home; machines cannot undergo the same.
- Processes refer to all the activities involved in the provision of goods and services to customers; processes are an element of capacity in terms of how much business an organization can *handle*.
- Supply capacity (purchases) is the ability to acquire the goods and services needed to operate. Supply capacity is harder to analyze, requiring an assessment of whether needed goods and services can reliably be acquired in the quantities, locations, and time frames needed.

### The CAM-I Model

As designed, the CAM-I capacity model focuses on physical capacity, though it can be modified to address other dimensions of capacity as well.

It begins with a notion of *rated capacity*, which is usually a 24/7/365 availability of physical resources. Time is the initial means of measurement. The rated capacity is then subdivided as follows:[7]

1. *Productive capacity*: capacity in use and providing salable goods and services—that is, revenue generating.
2. *Nonproductive capacity*: capacity in use but not providing salable goods or services.
3. *Idle capacity*: not currently in use.

We consider each of these categories, beginning with idle capacity.

## Idle Capacity

Capacity may be idle for various reasons. It may be *off limits*—that is, its use is prohibited by law, regulation, contract, physical limitations, or management decision. There may be certain hours of the day, or days of the week, when the business does not operate. Bars in some areas have opening and closing times set by law. A store in a shopping mall typically can operate only during hours when the mall itself is open. A golf course cannot function during nondaylight hours (unless the course is lighted) or during northern winters. Management is probably the prime mover in deciding to put capacity off limits by setting business hours, including deciding to be closed on certain days, not to work a third shift, and the like. Thus, some off-limit capacity may be mandatory, whereas others may be discretionary.

Capacity may be idle because it is deemed *nonmarketable*; that is, management believes that there is little or no demand to justify its use. There may not be enough product demand to justify a second or third shift, and so management leaves the plant idle during those times. A retail store may find too little demand during overnight hours to remain open 24 hours a day. Capacity may also be idle even though it is *potentially marketable*, but management chooses not to exploit the opportunity. A restaurant could be open for breakfast and lunch, but management chooses to operate a dinner-only facility. A company might be able to increase its marketing effort, thus creating more product demand to justify more production time, but it has not done so. Idle-marketable capacity suggests unexploited—though not necessarily profitable—revenue opportunities.

## Nonproductive Capacity

Capacity is nonproductive when it is in use but not producing salable goods and services. In a manufacturing environment, nonproductive may mean that the production facility is down for repair or maintenance, or that setup work is being performed. Production of defective goods also constitutes a nonproductive use of capacity. Often a major component of nonproductive use of capacity occurs when the business is open and staffed—the capacity is in use—but it is not fully productive because of a lack of customers. The restaurant with empty tables at dinnertime, the hotel with vacant rooms, and the airline with empty seats on a flight all demonstrate this type of nonproductive capacity, which may be called *stand-by capacity*. The physical facilities were designed to accommodate a given number of customers, but at some times, not enough customers are present.

Nonproductive time does not imply unnecessary time—it simply means non-revenue-generating time. Thus, for an airline, maintenance, loading and unloading, waiting for a connecting flight to arrive, and waiting to take off are necessary activities, but they do not generate revenue. Time spent in these activities means time not spent in moving passengers from place to place. Although nonproductive time can often be managed, it typically cannot be entirely eliminated.

## Productive Capacity

Capacity is productive when it generates revenue by producing salable goods and services. Having capacity in productive use is a desirable state, though incomplete. The capacity model is about the *utilization* of capacity but it says nothing about profitability. The goal of revenue management is to increase capacity utilization *and* be profitable.

The CAM-I model also includes as productive the capacity time spent on *product development*, such as running prototypes, and time spent on *process development*, such as integrating new equipment or techniques into production. Although these are not immediately revenue producing, they are deemed to contribute to future revenues by developing tomorrow's products and processes. The principle is stated as "the productive use of capacity results in tangible changes in the product or service that are of value to the customer."[8] Alternatively, one could classify these activities within the nonproductive-use-of-capacity category.

Some activities are difficult to classify, such as inspection and testing. Where each product is different, or where product failure would be catastrophic, as with elevator cables, aircraft, or military equipment, testing becomes an integral part of production and hence a productive use of capacity. Where production is more standardized or where failure of an individual unit has minor consequences, inspection and testing could be included as a nonproductive, albeit still necessary, use of capacity.[9]

## Example

Suppose a restaurant is open for dinner only, six days a week. Service hours are from 5:00 to 10:00 p.m., but the restaurant is staffed from 3:00 to 11:00 p.m. to allow for setup, initial food preparation, and cleaning. The physical capacity is available 168 hours per week (24 hours × 7 days). The productive capacity is at most 30 hours per week (5 hours × 6 days), depending on how full the restaurant is. The nonproductive time is at least 18 hours per week (the 3 hours daily of preparation and cleanup), plus any unutilized time during open hours. There remains 120 hours of idle time per week.

Suppose that the restaurant could serve 120 dinners each evening, given normal service durations. In a typical week, on average, 90 dinners are served daily, or 75 percent of maximum. The weekly capacity analysis is shown in Table 8.1.

### Using the Capacity Model to Enhance Revenues

The analysis of physical capacity utilization is a helpful tool for revenue management, by focusing attention on how the physical resources are used. But as pointed out earlier, the goal is not just increased utilization, but *profitable* utilization. Analyzing how much of a business's physical

*Table 8.1 Analysis of physical capacity*

| | | |
|---|---|---|
| Productive time (30 open hours × 75% utilization) | | 22.5 hours |
| Nonproductive time: stand-by capacity—restaurant is open and staffed but has unfilled space (30 hours × 25%) | 7.5 hours | |
| Nonproductive time: preparation and cleanup—restaurant is staffed but is not serving customers. | 18 hours | 25.5 hours |
| Idle capacity—restaurant is not in use | | 120 hours |
| Total time | | 168 hours |

*Note*: The physical facilities are in productive use about 13 percent of the available time, in nonproductive use about 15 percent of the available time, and idle about 71 percent of the available time.

capacity is idle or nonproductive can point to revenue enhancement opportunities.

Some businesses enhance revenues by expanding the use of only a portion of their physical resources. Many restaurants offer take-out or catering service, utilizing food-preparation capacity but not impacting dining room capacity. To the extent that the kitchen can handle more than the in-house customers, this approach is a good way to expand capacity utilization (by reducing nonproductive kitchen capacity) and enhance revenue. Similarly, many retailers offer catalog or online sales, further utilizing their inventory and distribution capacity beyond their retail store operations. This expansion enables the company to serve a new class of customers who are not close to a retail outlet, or who choose not to go to a physical site.

Analyzing how physical capacity is currently utilized—how much is idle and why, and how much is nonproductive and why—is a useful step to finding creative ways to enhance revenues without expanding one's investment in physical resources.

Issues in Measuring Physical Capacity Utilization

Early applications of revenue management were found primarily in industries that could easily measure utilization of physical capacity. An airline had a given number of seats on its flights, a hotel had a given number of rooms, and a restaurant had a reasonably given service capacity. Golf courses, theaters, cruise ships, rental car companies, and freight companies all have fairly well-defined notions of their service capacity and how much of it is being utilized. Manufacturing companies often have some idea of their maximum output capability, given their machines and process times, though varying product mix complicates the measure. Professional service firms, such as accountants and lawyers, would think more of the service capacity of their staff (discussed later) than of their physical resources. For some business types, however, the analysis of physical capacity is more challenging. How do we measure the utilization of the physical capacity of a retail store?

### Other Dimensions of Capacity

The CAM-I capacity model focuses on physical capacity, which is what the term *capacity* means to most people. Physical capacity is typically a major investment, is not easily or quickly modified, and represents a large fixed cost to most businesses. Considering how a company would increase the utilization of physical capacity for greater revenue and profit necessitates thinking about other dimensions of capacity as well. To make physical capacity operational typically requires personnel, purchases, and processes.

### Personnel

Personnel are almost always necessary to turn physical capacity into revenue. Aircraft cannot generate revenues without pilots, flight attendants, ground crew, and others. What differentiates personnel from physical assets is that personnel staffing is discretionary and often is capable of short-term modification. Although the physical facilities are in place 24/7/365, management decides how many personnel are in place at any given time. Thus, there is typically little notion of idle personnel capacity, in the sense that physical capacity can be idle. But there may be considerable nonproductive personnel capacity, especially of a stand-by nature—the business is open and staffed to serve customers, who may not materialize in the numbers expected. The CAM-I framework can be used to analyze the extent to which personnel capacity is productive or nonproductive.

Returning to the restaurant example earlier, assume that there are 18 employees—manager, cooks, other kitchen help, servers, clean-up personnel—all working from 3:00 to 11:00 p.m. The 144 daily hours of personnel capacity are analyzed in Table 8.2.

*Table 8.2 Analysis of personnel capacity (per day)*

| | | |
|---|---|---|
| Productive time (5 open hours × 18 staff × 75% utilization) | | 67.5 hours |
| Nonproductive time: stand-by capacity—restaurant is open and staffed but has unfilled space (5 hours × 18 × 25%) | 22.5 hours | |
| Nonproductive time: preparation and cleanup—restaurant is staffed but is not serving customers (3 hours × 18) | 54 hours | 76.5 hours |
| Idle capacity—restaurant is not in use (no staff on duty) | | 0 hours |
| Total time | | 144 hours per day |

Note: There is no idle capacity for personnel because the restaurant is not staffed at other times.

For some businesses, personnel capacity is far more important than physical capacity in determining revenue generation. Professional service firms, especially, sell the time of their professional staff rather than the utilization of their physical resources.

## Purchases

Beyond physical facilities and personnel, businesses require materials, supplies, and external services to generate revenue. Thus, purchases become an additional consideration. A dependable supply of such items—in the locations, quantities, and times needed—is critical to revenue generation. Some companies, such as Walmart, have extensive internal supply and distribution networks; others depend on a variety of external, independent suppliers.

## Processes

Finally, revenue generation depends on having sufficient processes in place to make the physical capacity, personnel, and purchases operational. Adequate information systems are an important process for many businesses; airlines and hotels depend on sophisticated reservation systems, which often allow price modifications to help fully utilize physical capacity.

The processes by which output is generated also impact capacity. For example, a restaurant's physical capacity depends on the size of its kitchen and dining area. Its personnel capacity depends on the number and capabilities of its food preparation and service personnel. The purchases dimension of its capacity reflects its ability to have a steady and reliable source of food and service products. But we cannot fully measure the restaurant's capacity without knowing something about its processes—is this restaurant a fast-food outlet, a buffet operation, casual dining, or fine dining? A fast-food restaurant has a greater customer capacity than a fine-dining restaurant, due to shorter preparation, service, and seating times—though it may not necessarily produce more revenue.

### Capacity Is a Multidimensional Concept

The previous example demonstrates that capacity is multidimensional. Physical capacity is the most constraining, because it is not easily changed in the short term. However, understanding how physical capacity is used—to what extent is it idle or nonproductive—is essential to revenue management. Converting some idle or nonproductive time to productive use may be a profitable way to enhance revenues without additional capital investment.

Physical capacity also may not be a single measure. Hotels have standard rooms and suites; an aircraft may have first-class and main-cabin seats. An airline may have different types of aircraft, and can decide which type to use on a given route, therefore affecting the capacity of that flight. A restaurant may have greater food preparation (kitchen) capacity than service (dining room) capacity, enabling it to consider adding take-out or catering services. The capacity of a manufacturing plant may depend on the mix of products being manufactured. Despite these complications, an analysis of how physical capacity is used is an important aspect of revenue management.

Processes may be the next most constraining feature of capacity, as they too are usually not easily changed. A business establishes and becomes known for the types of goods and services it provides—low cost or premium, minimal or high service, and other aspects of the business model. As noted earlier, processes impact the utilization of capacity and potential revenue generation.

Personnel and purchases are the most flexible dimensions of capacity. They also have considerable impact on revenue generation and profitability. Inadequate staffing or an inadequate supply of materials may lead to customers being turned away, or being unhappy with the quality of the goods or services provided. As mentioned earlier, Circuit City, a large consumer electronics chain, decided to lay off all its highest-paid floor personnel, in a misguided attempt to reduce costs and increase profitability. The results were disastrous from a revenue perspective. The remaining salespeople were young and inexperienced, and were unable to offer the technical information and advice customers needed. Customers were dissatisfied and took their business elsewhere, and the chain soon filed for bankruptcy. On the other hand, excessive staffing and an oversupply of materials add costs without generating revenue, and thus impair profitability. Making the right decisions on staffing and supply is critical to overall capacity management.

### Applying the CAM-I Model in Revenue Management

Capacity analysis is important to revenue management. Begin by applying the CAM-I model to physical capacity. How much of the time is capacity idle or nonproductive, and why? Can some of this idle or nonproductive time be converted to productive revenue-generating and profitable use?[10]

How does the business model—the processes for delivering goods and services—impact capacity? Are changes to these processes needed? And are the supporting processes, such as the information systems, adequate to support revenue growth?

Are personnel and supply reasonably aligned with capacity utilization—not too much, not too little? If some idle or nonproductive capacity can be made productive, are adequate personnel and supply sources available to service it?

There are numerous examples of companies employing their underutilized capacity to enhance their revenue generation, listed as follows:[11]

- Many supermarkets are open 24 hours. At one time, overnight hours were used solely for nonproductive maintenance and restocking tasks. The building was in use and had some staff. By adding some additional staffing (cashiers and a manager), sales could be made during these hours.
- Some fast-food establishments have instituted 24-hour service at their drive-through window. This service generates revenue with reduced staffing (no inside cleanup needed) and without compromising the safety and security of employees working overnight.
- Different parts of one's physical facilities may have different capacities. For example, a restaurant's kitchen may have sufficient space and personnel to prepare more meals than needed to serve dine-in patrons, given the seating capacity of the dining room and the pace of service. Many restaurants have increased utilization of their kitchen capacity and enhanced their revenue generation by offering take-out or catering service.
- Disney World adopted its FAST-PASS© system to reduce the waiting times for its attractions. Customers viewed waiting times as nonproductive because waiting reduced their enjoyment and might even discourage repeat visits. Disney also concluded that waiting time reduced customers' time to patronize other revenue-generating facilities, such as gift shops and eating establishments.
- Southwest Airlines attempts to achieve quick gate turnarounds; the time the aircraft spends at the gate is not revenue producing. By achieving quicker turns, an aircraft may be able to complete an additional flight each day.

Even though capacity considerations can be very complex in many business environments, it is difficult to effectively manage revenues without a good understanding of one's capacity and how it is being used. As a result of this analysis, new revenue opportunities may be uncovered.

# CHAPTER 9

# Revenue Management and the Theory of Constraints

Eli Goldratt popularized the theory of constraints (TOC) in his well-known instructional novel, *The Goal*. What he termed the TOC was a renewal and extension of the long-standing scarce resource problem in economics. The TOC concept offers insight into some revenue decisions and also expands the capacity concepts discussed in the preceding chapter.

## TOC Financial Measurement System

A very lean financial measurement system is one of the features of TOC. Goldratt argued that managers should focus on three measures, which he named *throughput, inventory*, and *operational expense.*

*Throughput* represents what the company generates through sales. It is typically measured as the revenue value of output less *truly variable* costs. Goldratt would argue that the only significant cost that is truly variable is the materials cost of the product. Some lesser costs that might also be truly variable could include sales commissions, if applicable, and perhaps power costs. But as a practical matter, throughput is measured as selling price minus materials, essentially a net revenue or value-added concept.

*Inventory* in a TOC system does *not* take on its usual accounting meaning of a stock of merchandise or materials. Rather, inventory represents *all* productive resources the company uses in order to operate and generate throughput. Thus, *inventory* includes inventories in the conventional sense, along with all other productive assets, both tangible and intangible: land, buildings, equipment, vehicles, technology, and so forth.

*Operational expense* is defined as all the costs needed to turn *inventory* into *throughput*, or all costs necessary to operate the enterprise. Labor, utilities, maintenance, insurance, selling and administrative, and similar costs are all grouped under the broad heading of *operational expense*.

The TOC financial measurement system has little use for the timing issues brought about by accrual accounting. Therefore, accounts receivable, accounts payable, accrued liabilities, and prepaid assets are not computed or considered. The system is close to cash accounting, and the focus is internal measurement, not external reporting. Similarly, issues of how the firm is financed are also ignored. Debt and equity financing, interest costs, and cost of capital are not considered.

In terms of desired outcomes, more throughput is preferred to less, and lower inventory and operational expense are preferred to higher amounts. Trade-offs are usually involved in any decision. An action is unambiguously good if it can increase throughput without increasing inventory and operational expense, or if it can decrease inventory or operational expense without decreasing throughput. In short, *improving one measure without harming the other two is desired*. When this ideal outcome cannot be achieved, the trade-offs need to be considered by management.

Note that the traditional applications of revenue management fit easily into this measurement context—to increase throughput (revenues net of any variable costs) without increasing the (fixed) operating cost base and without adding capacity (i.e., not increasing *inventory*). In the TOC context, *throughput* is king; the goal is to achieve more throughput while keeping *inventory* and *operational expense* under control. Achieving reductions in the latter two is desirable but secondary to growing throughput. In summary, TOC is very much a revenue management approach and only secondarily a cost management approach.

## Revenue Focus Versus Cost Focus

In *The Goal*, Goldratt tells the story of a plant manager struggling to keep his plant alive, because it is plagued with many of the problems of an aging manufacturing facility: high costs, large inventories, long lead times, and poor delivery performance. In their initial meeting, Alex Rogo (the plant manager) tells Jonah (the personification of Goldratt) about a new, highly automated machine recently installed in the plant. Alex insists that the new machine is really helping, and that efficiency measures are very impressive—high utilization and low unit costs. Jonah is skepti-cal, and correctly guesses that the plant continues to lose money, miss its delivery targets, and fail to get product out the door, while its invento-ries are skyrocketing. Jonah's guess correctly describes the situation, and his insight gets Alex's attention, as he faces a deadline to turn the plant around or have it closed. This encounter leads to a gradual but ongoing implementation of TOC principles that eventually saves the plant.

This episode leads to the first critical idea, namely that generating throughput (revenue management) is more important than cost reduction. Goldratt goes so far as to suggest that an excessive focus on efficiencies and cost management is actually harmful, because it distracts the management's attention from the key task of enhancing throughput. In the situation in the story, the automated machine's numbers, and indeed those for most of the plant's equipment, were good because machines and manpower were kept busy all the time doing *something*, resulting in high efficiency and favorable per-unit costs for the components being processed. But were they doing the right things? Some key component or assembly was often found to be lacking, which prevented shipping the customer's order on a timely basis. Meanwhile, the inventory of many other components was growing. The result was unhappy customers, low revenue, high costs, and a growing stockpile of raw materials, work in process, and some finished goods.

## Example of Excessive Cost Focus

You are the manager of a component production department within a large manufacturing company. Your department makes a single component, VG-7, which is used in assembling one of the company's major products. There are no other uses or external markets for VG-7. Further, your department is not equipped to make any other products. The assembly department tells you how many units of VG-7 are likely to be needed each day. These requirements are available to you, on an estimated basis, a month in advance. Estimates are typically quite close to actual requirements, which are provided weekly.

Operating costs for your department are $50,000 per day, including labor, machine costs, and other overhead—all costs except materials.

By union agreement, all employees work an eight-hour day, five days a week. They can be dismissed early, but are still paid for eight hours each day. Overtime is allowed, but one of your managerial objectives is to minimize overtime costs. In addition, you are judged on your daily cost per unit of the product. Your department works a single eight-hour shift, and is capable of producing 10,000 units of VG-7 per day. The material cost for VG-7 is one dollar per unit. A three-day inventory of VG-7 is maintained to allow for unforeseen production disruptions.

Today, after five hours of the eight-hour shift, your department has completed 6,250 units, which is all that assembly requires today. Your actual requirements for the coming week, and your estimated requirements for the coming month, are all in the range of 6,000 to 9,000 units daily. Your assistant asks if you wish to shut down the department for the day and send the employees home, or continue production for the remaining three hours.

This scenario represents a typical cost-focus situation. The decision on cost grounds would be to continue working. If employees are sent home after five hours, today's unit cost of VG-7 would be nine dollars per unit:

$$Producing\ 6{,}250\ units\ costs\ \$50{,}000 + (6{,}250 \times \$1) =$$
$$\$56{,}250\ or\ \$9\ per\ unit$$

Continuing to work for the full eight hours will reduce that unit cost to six dollars per unit:

$$Producing\ 10{,}000\ units\ costs\ \$50{,}000 + (10{,}000 \times \$1) =$$
$$\$60{,}000\ or\ \$6\ per\ unit$$

Although producing 10,000 units at a unit cost of $6 may seem more attractive, such a decision would violate TOC principles. Since today's demand for this component is 6,250 units, no additional revenue (throughput) can be generated by producing more units of VG-7. Further, production requirements for the foreseeable future are well below the 10,000-unit-per-day capacity of the department, and an inventory exists to cover unforeseen emergencies. Because there is no need to build inventory, the best decision is to stop today's production at 6,250 units. This decision is consistent with the principles of *The Goal*, in that continuing production to 10,000 units per day increases *inventory*, probably increases *operational expense* at least to the extent of holding costs for the additional inventory, but leaves *throughput* unchanged.

Using average cost as a performance metric, as just seen, is generally a bad idea because it encourages the behavior of full *activation* of resources, whether productive or not. One of the principles of TOC is that *activating* a resource (having it perform work) is not the same as *utilizing* the resource (generating throughput). Indeed, under TOC, most resources (including human ones) should *not* be working all the time. It is virtually impossible to have exactly the right amount of each capacity resource; resources should be activated only to the extent that they generate throughput. Thus, the company is better off by idling the department after five hours, even if employees are paid for a full eight-hour shift.

## The Presence of Constraints

Central to the TOC is the notion that a revenue-generation system must face one or more *constraints*—limitations on its throughput capacity. If constraints did not exist, throughput could increase without limit, which we observe is not the case. A constraint is any factor that limits throughput. The constraint may be physical (an element of productive capacity or some limitations on availability of materials), external (lack of sufficient demand), or policy based (managerially imposed, such as a single-shift operation). Thus, a typically full aircraft route faces a physical constraint (lack of more seats), whereas an aircraft route only 50 percent full faces a market constraint (lack of demand or perhaps lack of sales effort).

Although one or more constraints on throughput necessarily exist, Goldratt would argue that relatively few are active at any one time, thus making it possible to actively manage the constraints.

### Revenue Management Under Constraint Conditions

Managing revenues (throughput) in the face of constraints involves the five-step process outlined in *The Goal*:[1]

1. Identify the current constraint(s). What factors are currently limiting throughput or revenue generation?

2. Decide how to generate the most throughput from the constraint. An illustration follows in the next section.

3. Subordinate everything else to the earlier decision. Throughput is king; do not be distracted by other goals.

4. Seek ways to relax or bypass (*elevate*) the constraint. How can more throughput be generated in the face of the current constraint?

5. If, via the preceding process, a constraint is eliminated, return to Step 1, find the new constraint, and go through the process again. Beware of inertia, of thinking that once a constraint is removed, the problem has been solved.

### *Example of Managing Throughput Under Constraint Conditions*

Walden's Wide World of Furniture manufactures unfinished furniture.[2] A small production unit in Jamestown specializes in two items: an end table and a footstool. These are just two of many items that Walden produces, but they are the only items produced in the Jamestown facility.

For each item—end tables (ET) and footstools (FS)—the manufacturing process involves three machines: a table saw (Department A), a jigsaw (Department B), and a sander (Department C). Jamestown has two of each of these machines and one operator for each machine; the operators are not cross-trained. After the component pieces are made by processing on each of the machines as needed, the item is put together by the assembly department (Department D). The Jamestown site thus has four production resources and two employees in each department.

ET sell for $90 each, and Walden can sell up to 200 units per week. Raw material for an end table consists of one piece of 1-inch round maple stock, which costs $18, and one piece of 12 inch × 16 inch × 1 inch maple, which costs $20. Production and assembly are relatively simple:

- The round maple stock begins in the table saw department (A) where it is cut into pieces for the legs in 15 minutes. Then the legs are sanded (C) for 10 minutes.

- The 12 × 16 × 1 piece goes to the jigsaw (B) and is shaped, taking 15 minutes. The shaped piece then requires five minutes to sand (C).
- Finally, all pieces go to Department D where they are assembled using small metal brackets (cost is $6 per set); assembly takes 10 minutes. Total production time for an end table is 55 minutes.

FS sell for $100 each; at most, 100 of these are sold each week. Each footstool requires one piece of the 12 × 16 × 1 maple and one piece of 2-inch round pine stock, which together cost $18. As with the ET, production and assembly are relatively simple:

- The 12 × 16 × 1 piece goes to Department B and is shaped, requiring 15 minutes.
- The shaped piece then is sanded in five minutes (C). (This is identical to the piece that is used in ET.)
- The round pine stock goes to the table saw (A) and is cut into pieces for the legs; this step takes 10 minutes.
- The legs now go to the jigsaw (B) where notches are cut for the cloth upholstery, taking 15 minutes. (The legs are not sanded, because they will be hidden by the upholstery; Walden sells this product as unfinished furniture, without the upholstery.)
- All pieces then go to assembly (D), which takes five minutes. The total production time for a footstool is 50 minutes.

Each department employee works a guaranteed 40 hours per week and receives pay and benefits equal to $15 per hour. It costs a total $11,200 per week to operate the plant, including the supervisor's salary, wages and benefits of the eight production workers, heat, lights, rent, and so on.

The supervisor currently faces two problems. First, headquarters has just instituted a new planning process and, as part of this process, she must submit a profit target for next week. Second, an engineering student intern from Jamestown Community College just presented her with his report in which he recommends purchasing a different type of jigsaw. The new equipment would cost $10,000 and would reduce the time for

Department B to shape each piece from 15 minutes to 14 minutes, but unfortunately would increase the time for Department C to sand each piece from 5 minutes to 7 minutes.

The supervisor prepared an initial weekly budget, based on the production and sale of 200 ET and 100 FS, the maximum projected demand for these products. Her budget resulted in a projected profit of $4,200. The projected profit seemed a little high, but she checked her figures and everything seemed fine. She noted that her budgeted production required 266.67 hours of production labor (see later for this calculation), well below the 320 hours available. She also wondered whether she should use the extra time to produce some tables or FS for inventory, as Walden was about to begin a new advertising campaign for its products in the hope of increasing demand.

As the supervisor tried to decide what profit figure she should commit to for the next week, she also tried to figure out how to tell her intern that his recommendation unfortunately ignored a critical variable, product cycle time, and that what she needed was a way to reduce the time required to produce ET and FS, not increase it.

Analysis and Discussion

This case is designed to illustrate the TOC principles set forth in *The Goal.* The following are the five steps of managing in the face of constraints:

1. Identify the constraint.
2. Decide how to exploit (get the most out of) the constraint.
3. Subordinate everything else to Step 2.
4. Attempt to elevate the constraint.
5. If a constraint is broken, return to Step 1.

Walden is a two-product, four-process situation. Fixed capacities exist for the four processes (80 hours each, per week).

*Recreate the Supervisor's Budget*    The budget is based on maximum output (market demand) for both ET and FS

### Revenue:

| 200 ET at $90 | $18,000 |
|---|---|
| 100 FS at $100 | $10,000 |
| Total | $28,000 |

### Expenses:

| Materials | Labor and overhead | Materials + labor and overhead |
|---|---|---|
| 200 ET at $44: $8,800 | $11,200 | $23,800 |
| 100 FS at $38: $3,800 | | |
| Total materials: $12,600 | | |
| *Projected profit (revenues − expenses)* | $4,200 | |

### Time required for production:

| 200 ET at 55 minutes | 11,000 minutes |
|---|---|
| 100 FS at 50 minutes | 5,000 minutes |
| Total | 16,000 minutes = 266.67 hours |

Note: The total time calculated is less than the 320 hours available, so it seems feasible.

The initial budget shows an expected profit of $4,200, based on planned maximum production of each product (200 ET and 100 FS). Although there was enough *total* time to achieve this output, no account was taken of the time required on a process-by-process basis.

*Diagram the Production Process*    In a simple situation, diagramming the process as shown in Figure 9.1 may be sufficient to identify the constraint. Note that the steps involving Raw Material 2 (RM2) were common to both products. In more complex situations, determining the constraint(s) may not be so easy.

*What Is the Constraint in the Process?*    Determine how much time each product requires of each resource, then show the maximum weekly output of that product that can be achieved with each resource (see Table 9.1).

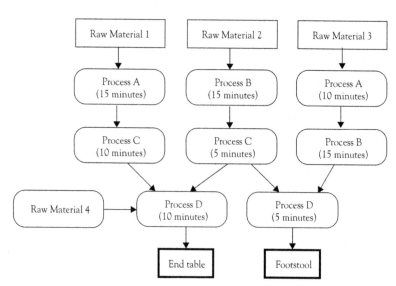

**Figure 9.1 Diagram of production process**

**Table 9.1 Identify constrained resource**

| Resource (80 hours of each) | Time per footstool (minutes) | Time per end table (minutes) | Maximum ET possible | Maximum FS possible |
|---|---|---|---|---|
| A | 15 | 10 | 320 | 480 |
| B | 15 | 30 | 320 | 160 |
| C | 15 | 5 | 320 | 960 |
| D | 10 | 5 | 480 | 960 |

With respect to ET, A, B, and C are equally constraining, limiting production to 320 ET; D has the capacity to do more. For the FS, B is the constraint, limiting production to 160 FS, while A, C, and D could produce more. Note that all four resources are needed to produce a product; so output is limited by the most constrained resource. In this situation, *B is the constraint.*

*Comment:* Here we identified the constraint, thus satisfying Step 1. Process B turned out to be the constraint, the step in the production process that limited total output.

*Does Enough Capacity Exist to Meet the Supervisor's Schedule?*    No. Production of 200 ET and 100 FS requires 100 hours (6,000 minutes) of resource B, and we have only 80 hours. The 6,000 minutes of resource B needed is calculated as follows.

| 200 ET at 15 minutes | 3,000 minutes |
|---|---|
| 100 FS at 30 minutes | 3,000 minutes |
| | 6,000 minutes or 100 hours |

*Comment:* There was not enough time in process B to produce 200 ET and 100 FS. Although processes A, C, and D had sufficient capacity (time), the budgeted output could not be completed and sold (throughput) without the work required in process B. Full output of both products required 100 hours of B, and Walden has only 80. Thus, the supervisor must decide on the mix of products, as full output of both products was impossible under current conditions.

*A Tentative Production Plan Based on Product Profitability*    One way to select a production plan in the face of a constraint is to emphasize the production of the most profitable product. Thus, we first calculate the per-unit profitability of each product by conventional accounting means (see Table 9.2).

This analysis indicates that FS are clearly the more profitable product; so the tentative production plan is to maximize the output of FS (100).

**Table 9.2 Product profitability**

| | ET ($) | FS ($) |
|---|---|---|
| Revenue per unit | 90.00 | 100.00 |
| Materials per unit | (44.00) | (38.00) |
| Contribution margin, or throughput | 46.00 | 62.00 |
| Labor: $15/hour × (55/60) | (13.75) | (12.50) |
| Overhead: $20*/hour × (55/60) | (18.33) | (18.33) |
| **Per-unit profit** | 13.92 | 31.17 |

*Labor and overhead amount to $11,200 per week, of which labor is $15 per hour for 320 hours, or $4,800 in total. Subtracting $4,800 from $11,200 leaves $6,400 for overhead. If overhead is assigned on a per-hour basis (a common method), then the overhead rate is $6,400/320 hours, or $20 per labor hour.

This output requires 50 hours of Department B, leaving 30 hours for the production of ET, enough for 120 ET to be produced. Thus, the production plan is 120 ET and 100 FS.

*Comment:* The first pass at selecting how much of each product to produce was based on determining which product was more profitable, using conventional accounting. FS were clearly the more profitable product; so the production plan is to produce 100 FS (the maximum demand) and 120 ET. This decision took account of the constraint in process B, by having a total production that was achievable in the 80 hours of B available. But, as will be seen, it did not assure that we had yet identified the best use of B, even though we were maximizing what appeared to be the more profitable product.

*What Is the Expected Profit from This Plan?*

| | |
|---|---|
| 120 ET at $90 − $44 = 120 × $46 | $5,520 |
| 100 FS at $100 − $38 = 100 × $62 | $6,200 |
| Total | $11,720 |
| Operating costs | ($11,200) |
| Net profit | $520 |

*Comment:* The profit outcome from the initial production plan (100 FS and 120 ET) is a weekly profit of $520, far less than the original $4,200!

*Is There a Better Plan?*    To get the best outcome, we should maximize the throughput ($T$) value of the constrained resource, B. We can calculate B's throughput per minute:

If B makes ET, $T = \$46$ and 15 minutes are needed per unit:
$$\$46T/15 \text{ minutes} = \$3.066T \text{ per minute}$$

If B makes FS, $T = \$62$ and 30 minutes are needed per unit:
$$\$62T/30 \text{ minutes} = \$2.067T \text{ per minute}$$

B's time is more valuable when making ET, and the new production plan should be to maximize the output of ET (200). This output requires

50 hours of Department B, leaving 30 hours for the production of FS, and 60 FS could be produced. The revised production plan is 200 ET and 60 FS.

*Comment:* We introduce a new metric, the *throughput value per unit of the constrained resource.* It is a reasonable answer to the question of how to get the most out of the constraint (Step 2). FS had a throughput value of $62 ($100 selling price minus $38 material cost), and we needed 30 minutes of B to produce one footstool. B generates throughput at the rate of $2.067 per minute ($62/30 minutes) when producing FS. ET had a throughput value of only $46, but each table needs only 15 minutes of process B; so B generates a throughput value of $3.066 per minute ($46/15 minutes) when producing ET. Thus, producing ET is a better use of the constrained resource than producing FS, which suggests a production plan that maximizes end-table production. This conclusion led to a new plan of producing 200 ET (the maximum demand) and 50 FS, again fully utilizing B's time.

*What Is the Expected Profit from the Revised Plan?*

| 200 ET at $90 − $44 = 200 × $46 | $9,200 |
|---|---|
| 60 FS at $100 − $38 = 60 × $62 | $3,720 |
| Total | $12,920 |
| Operating costs | ($11,200) |
| Net profit | $1,720 |

*Comment:* The revised plan yields a profit of $1,720, compared to $520 for the prior plan, or a $1,200 profit improvement. This analysis suggests that, in the face of constraints, one should make decisions by *maximizing the throughput value of the constraint.*

*The Intern's Proposal*    The proposal is to buy a piece of equipment for $10,000 that would reduce B's process time (for both functions that B performs) from 15 minutes to 14 minutes, and would increase C's time to process RM2 from 5 minutes to 7 minutes. B is currently able to process 200 ET and 60 FS in the 80 available hours (4,800 available minutes). This change would reduce B's time from 15 to 14 minutes for ET and from 30 to 28 minutes for FS.

| 200 ET at 14 minutes | 2,800 minutes |
|---|---|
| 60 FS at 28 minutes | 1,680 minutes |
| Total | 4,480 minutes |

Current production would thus require only 4,480 minutes of B's time. The 320 minutes that are freed up by this change could be used to produce additional FS. In 320 minutes, B could produce 11.4 (11 in whole numbers) more FS per week. This added production would generate an additional throughput of $682 (= 11 × $62) per week. The additional time required for C is costless since C has enough excess capacity to handle the additional time required.

*Comment:* This part of the scenario illustrates Step 4, attempting to relax or *elevate* the constraint. The proposal saves a minute in process B at a cost of two more minutes in process C. Although increasing total production time may initially seem unappealing, a closer look shows that Walden is saving time on the constraint (B)—which will permit an increase in throughput—while the added time on process C doesn't matter since Walden is not fully utilizing that resource and thus has plenty of excess capacity. Assuming that Walden saves a minute in both of B's actions (shaping the 12 × 16 × 1 maple, which applies to both products, and notching the pine legs), then the earlier production plan of 200 ET and 60 FS, which had used all 4,800 minutes of B's time before, would now require only 4,480 minutes, freeing up 320 minutes of B's time, which can be used to produce more FS (Walden is already producing the maximum demand of ET). With 320 minutes now available, at 28 minutes per footstool, Walden could produce 11.4 more per week. Rounding down to 11 additional FS, at a $62 throughput value each, would generate an additional $682 profit weekly, which would pay for the $10,000 new machine in about 15 weeks. Thus, the proposed change, even though requiring a $10,000 investment and expanding the total processing time, would be beneficial.

## Conclusion

The theory of constraints has much to offer for revenue management. Throughput, or net revenue, is the major metric in a TOC system, and most decisions emphasize the ability to generate more throughput and to do so efficiently. A strategy of maximizing throughput without increasing operational expense or inventory is a strategy of profitable revenue growth. Further, the notion of maximizing the throughput of constrained resources strengthens the link between revenue management and capacity, as developed in the preceding chapter. Although analyzing constraints and applying TOC concepts require a thorough and detailed analysis, improved management of revenues and increases in profit can result.

# CHAPTER 10

# Relating Revenue Management to Customer Value

One theme in cost analysis has direct linkage to revenue management, namely the effort to classify costs as value-added or non-value-added costs. Value-added costs are those that provide something for which a customer is willing to pay. This concept has a direct role in revenue management; customers are willing to pay for the *value* they receive from a purchase.

Early research by McNair and Vangermeersch analyzed profitability as four concentric circles.[1] The inner circle represents a core of activities that adds value to the company's products or services. These activities may contribute to the functional characteristics of the product or service, their quality, customer support services, company reputation, timely delivery, and price. Surrounding these value-added costs are non-value-added but necessary costs. These costs do not contribute to the customer's benefit but are required to run the business. The next circle is that of non-value-added and unnecessary costs, termed *waste*. The outer ring is the company's profit, which is bounded by limitations on its ability to charge higher prices.

In subsequent research, the terms *non-value-added* costs and *waste* did not sit well with managers of those functions. The previous three cost categories were revised to the following five.[2]

1. Value-added costs, which directly benefit a customer.
2. Business value-added costs—current, which do not directly affect customer satisfaction (unless done poorly, such as billing).

3. Business value-added costs—future, which create the company's future products or services, growth, and competitive position.

4. Business value-added costs—administrative, which are needed to support the firm and its management.

5. Non-value-added costs, which have no stakeholder benefits and thus should be minimized or eliminated (formerly termed *waste*).

Value-added costs may be further subdivided, according to McNair, Polutnik, and Silvi (2000), into *table stakes* and *revenue enhancers*.[3] *Table stakes* involves the costs of providing the basic features a customer would expect in a product or services; these are required to be a player in the industry.[4] *Revenue enhancers* are the costs of the extra product or service features that differentiate a company's offerings from those of its competitors.

## The Discount Phenomenon

Providing customer value is central to revenue management; however, much of the development in recent years has been at the low end of the value scale. Shell traces the history, expansion, and widespread implications of a discounting culture in her book, *Cheap: The High Cost of Discount Culture*.[5] The concept of discount stores is not new. One of the earliest, John Wanamaker & Co., dates to the 1860s. Their large stores enabled purchasing in bulk, hence giving a pricing advantage over the small retailers of the day. Wanamaker is also credited with inventing the price tag, changing retailing from negotiated prices to pre-established prices.[6] In 1878, Frank W. Woolworth opened the first 5 and 10 store, featuring inexpensive merchandise. He pioneered the change from clerk service (goods behind the counter) to self-service (goods on open display), gaining a price advantage by requiring fewer—and less-skilled—workers. Eventually, Woolworth expanded into manufacturing as well, achieving further price reductions by emulating European mass production techniques.[7] Other similar stores, such as W. T. Grant and S. S. Kresge, soon followed. In 1895, Richard Sears took another step toward lower prices by beginning a catalog mail-order retailer, thus reducing the need for, and cost of, retail outlets and giving the company an instant national presence.

The post–World War II period saw the growth of the large suburban discount store, which followed the mass migration of the population from cities to suburbs. Kmart, Target, Woolco, and others emerged, and then, later, Walmart. Again, various cost savings drove prices down.

Besides bulk purchasing and labor savings, the stores were located in lower-cost areas, forcing customers to drive some distance to shop there. Shoppers had to accumulate their purchases and bring them to cashiers at the front of the store, and little service was available in the merchandise aisles. Moreover, the variety of merchandise was more limited than that in a full-service department store. More tasks were transferred to the customer, often including the assembly of merchandise.[8]

The outlet mall developed initially as a way for manufacturers to dispose of imperfect or excess products, initially in *factory stores*. Later, these were grouped together as outlet malls. Located in remote areas, sometimes between major cities, these locations required considerable travel. Unlike many discount stores, outlet malls offered top brand names at reduced prices, despite the risks of degrading the brand name by discounting. More recently, *dollar stores* have become increasingly prevalent, not limited to poorer neighborhoods. It is evident that there is considerable demand for low cost, and sometimes lower quality, merchandise.

Much of the success in discount operations depends on tight cost management: using buying power, keeping labor costs low, maintaining low-cost and efficient distribution and retail operations, and making maximum use of information. Yet, the revenue management side is important as well, identifying merchandise that will sell in volume, and pricing that merchandise at a profitable level. Discount stores are not necessarily low profit; Walmart is one of the country's most successful businesses. As Shell states, "It seems that the poor benefit the discounting industry far more than the discounting industry benefits the poor."[9]

The notion of providing customer value, however, extends beyond selling at low prices. Indeed, a focus on customer value is often considered as a way of maintaining prices in a culture that emphasizes discounting. The companies just mentioned found ways to add customer value, often by reducing non-value-added costs, which in turn reduced consumer prices. Those who managed revenues and costs successfully have thrived.

## Types of Buyers

In considering customer value as a revenue management strategy, one must understand actual and potential customers, their preferences, and their motivations. This section addresses different types of buyers and revenue management strategies appropriate to each. It is said that there are four types of buyers:[10]

1. *Price buyers* make decisions strictly on price. They maintain a variety of suppliers and have little to no supplier loyalty.
2. *Value buyers* make decisions on broader criteria, including the impact of purchases on their operations and customers. They tend to maintain longer supplier relationships, and interact with suppliers on enhancing the cost-effectiveness of both parties.
3. *Relationship buyers* value long-term connections with their suppliers, which they feel will lead to superior service and support.
4. *Perennial negotiators* are motivated to see how low a price they can achieve, even on nonstandard products and services. They often see negotiating the lowest possible price as a challenge.

Original applications of revenue management focused on customers who were price buyers. The earliest users offered price reductions to entice price-sensitive buyers to situations where excess supply—especially perishable supply—existed. Price buyers can be profitable customers, if properly managed. Managing the price buyer was the theme of early revenue management, establishing restrictions on the availability of price reductions and trying to minimize the migration of regular customers to the reduced price offerings.

A greater variety of revenue management options is available for dealing with customers who are value buyers or relationship buyers, as factors other than price enter into the purchase decision. These types of customers can be the most profitable. The following sections discuss the notion of providing customer value.

Perennial negotiators, called *poker-playing buyers* by one writer, are probably best avoided, as they are the least likely to generate profitable business, either for individual sales transactions or as long-run customers.[11]

## What Is Customer Value?

This section discusses determining what is valued by customers and then managing product decisions to optimize revenue and overall profitability.

Customer value is generally the savings and satisfaction that a customer receives from the purchase of a product or service. Zeithaml defined customer value as consisting of low price, receiving what was expected, and product or service quality commensurate with price.[12] Dube and Shoemaker identified six dimensions of value:[13]

- Financial (current price, future savings, money back if not satisfied);
- Temporal (time savings);
- Functional (availability of desired services);
- Experiential (quality of the experience, especially in establishments such as restaurants);
- Emotional (recognition and more pleasurable experiences); and
- Social (a personal linkage with the provider).

Different customers will attach different weights and values to these dimensions.

In business-to-business selling, customer value is whatever supports the financial and operating priorities and needs of the customer. Although low price certainly falls in this category, customers may also find value in the following services and support:

- Ready availability of products and services;
- Reliable delivery dates;
- Responsive service, availability of parts, or both;
- Reliability of operations or technology; minimal downtime;
- Geographical convenience for service and support;
- Available options for customization; and
- Favorable credit terms.

Determining customer value means understanding the customer, the customer's business, and what the customer needs to do to be successful. Interaction with customers is helpful in determining what they value. Ask them what they need, offer it, and provide it.

In consumer selling, customer value may be broader, fulfilling a variety of customer needs or desires. Customers may find value in the following nonprice areas:

- Availability of variety (colors, sizes, etc.);
- Ease of use;
- Preassembly, or ease of assembly;
- Technical support;
- Availability of, and ease of, a return privilege;
- Availability of service;
- Availability of the latest style, technology, and so on.

Determining what consumers value is more difficult than determining what business customers value. Consumers' tastes and needs change, and are driven by a variety of motivations. Keeping in touch with customer markets, such as seniors, college students, high earners, or other relevant groups, is essential to anticipate what tomorrow's customer will value. Detailed transaction analysis may also be helpful in early identification of trends.

### Revenue Management of Customer Value

Using customer value in revenue management usually requires having a range of product and service offerings, to be able to match to the price willingness and business needs of the customer. One can then add or subtract value features—services and product enhancements—to allow for price flexibility.

One author suggests that there be a minimum of three levels of the product or service offering:[14]

1. A core offering, with a minimum set of features to make the product or service usable by a large number of customers. This offering will appeal to the most price-sensitive customers.
2. One or more *expected offerings*, adding product features, support services, or other elements of the transaction (such as credit terms or delivery promises) desired by many customers.
3. Value-added options that meet the needs of specific customers.

For example, TurboTax®, Intuit's popular income tax preparation software, offers six versions:[15]

1. Free, capable of completing the most basic income tax return (1040EZ or 1040A). This base product is offered free, presumably as an inducement to consider higher-level programs in the future. The free product is available for online use only, and free access to an online state program is also provided.
2. Basic ($19.99 download or CD), for individual taxpayers with a range of fairly common income items.
3. Deluxe ($34.99 online/$59.99 download or CD), for individual taxpayers who seek to maximize their deductions and require assistance to ensure that all deductions are claimed.
4. Premier ($54.99/$89.99), for individual taxpayers with investments and rental property.
5. Home and Business ($79.99/$99.99), for individual taxpayers with an unincorporated business or single-owner limited liability company (LLC).
6. Business ($149.99), for corporations, partnerships, and LLCs.

Although bundles and options change frequently, online options for the Deluxe, Premier, Home and Business, and Business versions do not include software for state taxes, which is available for an additional fee, according to the customer's needs. The download or CD price, except for the basic version, includes state software. These extensive options are an attempt by Intuit, the provider of TurboTax, to tailor purchase options to different customer needs. These six versions serve a range of customer situations.

As an example of providing a much greater degree of customization, consider the wide range of options offered by Disney World for tickets to its attractions:[16]

- One-day to 10-day passes good for admission to a single theme park each day, at per-day prices ranging from $99 to $35.40 ($354 total), with the pass expiring 14 days from the first use.

- A *park-hopper* option, providing admission to as many as four theme parks on the same day, at a flat price of $60 in addition to the basic ticket price, whether attached to a 1-day or 10-day ticket.

- A *water park fun & more* option, providing one additional admission per day to any of seven added attractions, at the same price as the park-hopper option.

- Both the *park-hopper* and the *water park fun & more* options at a flat price of $86 in addition to the basic ticket price, whether attached to a 1-day or 10-day ticket.

- A *no expiration* option (unused days never expire, thus can be used beyond the 14-day limit of the base pass). The price for this option is no longer shown on the website, and is available only by phone call.

- An annual pass priced at $634, featuring a year of unlimited admission to the four theme parks, free parking, and other amenities.

- A premium annual pass priced at $754, which adds a year's unlimited access to water parks, a golf course, and other attractions to the basic annual pass.

The various combinations of number of days and the add-on options create a large number of customizable choices for the buyer.

## Conclusion

Providing customer value is an important basis for differential pricing. Note that differential pricing does not mean charging what the customer is willing to pay, as different prices for identical product or service packages will engender customer ill will in the long run. Rather, it means being able to configure a combination of product features, services, and transaction terms that meets the needs of a particular customer. Providing such value also engenders confidence on the seller's part, an important defense against the constant pressure for discounting.

# CHAPTER 11

# Are Your Customers Profitable?

Not all customers are good customers. Eliminating unprofitable or marginally profitable customers is a component of effective revenue management. Many sellers are not particularly discriminating; one author reports that 79 percent of business-to-business companies respond to all customers.[1] There may be a cost to responding to all customers because optimal revenue management seeks customers who will result in *profitable* sales. This chapter discusses how to assess which customers are valuable and which are not.

The 80/20 rule is well known: In general, 80 percent of one's business will come from 20 percent of customers. This rule does not imply that one should pay attention only to big customers, many of whom may be *price buyers*, adept at obtaining price concessions. Smaller customers may be more likely to be *value buyers* or *relationship buyers* who may need, and be willing to pay for, value enhancements and support services.

The key question is not only how much revenue does a customer generate but how much does it cost to service that customer? Harvard professors Robin Cooper and Robert Kaplan have proposed the 20/225 rule. They studied one company where 20 percent of the customers provided 225 percent of profits, 70 percent of customers were more or less break-even, and the remaining 10 percent of customers *lost* 125 percent of profits.[2] Whether these percentages apply in other situations or not, every business has some customers who cost more to serve than they generate in revenues. These customers may successfully negotiate lower prices, buy low-value products and services, require excessive support, change orders on short notice, be slow paying, or evidence any number of other characteristics that are costly to the seller. The first goal is to convert unprofitable customers to profitable ones, which may require interaction with the customer to get them to change their costly behaviors. The ultimate option, if customers cannot be moved to the profitable category, is to terminate them. Faced with such an ultimatum, some customers may revise their behaviors, and those who will not are best left to one's competitors.

## One Company's Experience

Kanthal is currently a brand of heating and technology service products for the Swedish company, the Sandvik Group. It provides furnace products and heating systems, materials in wire and strip form, resistors and capacitors, along with various technical services.[3] In 1988, it served as a subject for a Harvard Business School case study on its experiences with customer profitability analysis.[4] The company was then a part of the Kanthal–Hoganas group. At that time, it had about 15,000 items in its product line, and it served about 10,000 customers.

To assess customer profitability, the company used activity-based costing techniques to analyze its selling and administrative expenses. These costs, which represented about 34 percent of total company costs, had previously been largely ignored. To the extent they were considered at all in pricing, they were applied as a flat percentage of sales revenue. The company felt, however, that individual customers made varying demands on their sales and administrative resources. They described high-profit and low-profit customers as follows:

- Low-profit customers place high demands on technical and commercial service. They buy low margin products in small orders. Frequently, they order nonstandard products that have to be specially produced for them. And we have to supply special selling discounts in order to get the business.
- High-profit customers buy high-margin, standard products in large orders. They make no demands for technical or commercial service, and accurately forecast for us their annual demands.[5]

The company analyzed its production, selling, and administrative costs in two categories: those related to a customer order and those related to manufacturing volume. Various product lines, customers, and customer groups were studied. All analyses found a wide range of outcomes, with some orders or customers showing high profitability and others a large loss. Its analysis of in-country (Swedish) customers showed that only 40 percent were profitable, and that these, in fact, generated 250 percent of profits, whereas the least profitable 10 percent of customers lost 120 percent of profits.[6] The original expectation that low-volume customers were likely to be unprofitable was not always borne out. Two of the company's largest-volume customers were shown to be unprofitable. These customers had adopted just-in-time systems, which required frequent shipments and placed huge demands on Kanthal's production and order-filling operations.

### How to Respond?

Kanthal's findings then raised the question of what to do. The actions taken by this company are illustrative of possible actions to change unprofitable orders into profitable ones:[7]

- Simplify product lines. For one line, Kanthal reduced the number of available sizes from 10 to 3.
- Set minimum order sizes for custom products. Kanthal decided to accept small orders only for stocked products.
- Service smaller accounts through distributors, rather than directly.
- Work with large customers having special needs to find more effective ways of meeting their requirements. Kanthal installed online order systems for the just-in-time customers to facilitate smooth information flow.
- Work with customers to reduce their high-cost behaviors. Kanthal gave one customer a five percent price reduction when that customer reduced the number of order lines by half. This action more than doubled the customer's profitability.
- If all else fails, consider dropping the customer.

Actions such as these may not fully solve the problem; orders and customers generating losses may remain, but their numbers should be reduced and overall performance should improve.

## The Difficulty of Customer Analysis

Calculating customer profitability is no easy task. The starting point is straightforward: How much does the customer buy (gross revenue), and what is the cost of the goods or services sold to that customer? Price adjustments such as discounts or extended terms are fairly easy to analyze, along with the costs of certain specialized services such as particular packing and shipping requirements. Other elements of customer profitability are harder to analyze. How much extra cost is incurred for a customer who places frequent small orders or who orders a great variety of items in small quantities? What does it cost to field technical information or assistance requests from a customer? How much extra do orders for nonstandard products cost? How much time does the sales staff spend with a given customer and at what cost? Incorporating elements such as these into customer profitability analysis requires specialized cost studies, which may be both costly and imprecise. But even if one is unable to quantify all the costs of servicing each customer, a partial attempt is still informative.

## The Importance of Customer Analysis

As the Harvard case study demonstrated, a company can manage revenues and optimize profits if it gathers and analyzes customer data. Many companies (a) lack the capability to analyze customer profitability; (b) do not take the time to carry out this analysis; or (c) do not believe that the assessment will result in higher profits after considering the cost to collect and analyze the data.

If the 20/225 rule proposed by Cooper and Kaplan, or something close to it, indeed applies to many companies, managers should try to identify which customers are the major profit drivers, and which customers constitute a drain on profits. A good company information system can be an excellent way to collect such data.

There are many examples of companies that do not seem to effectively manage their revenues by assessing valuable versus unprofitable customers. For example, one could consider the last time the customer ordered. A common example is a gift order for a child from a mail order company's catalog. That customer is likely to continue to receive costly mailings from that company for many years, even though the recipient may no longer be a viable customer because the child has advanced beyond the age of the company's products. Further, the common practice of sharing mailing lists will result in that customer receiving mailings from many other suppliers, who may never receive an order. A customer information system might report (a) if this customer ever placed an order; (b) if so, how many orders; (c) how long ago the last order occurred; and (d) whether the order was sufficiently profitable. Customers who may have placed a single order long ago and have not ordered since then should probably be dropped from the mailing list.

Some years ago, a national public accounting firm analyzed its customer base in a smaller city. They had two large, profitable customers there and many smaller, much less profitable customers. The firm decided to drop many of these smaller customers. While the firm addressed the profitability of individual customers, it needed to take into account the overall picture as well. Many of the smaller clients were not-for-profit organizations, which had June 30 fiscal years compared to the December 31 fiscal years for the large clients. Although they were less profitable, these clients did generate revenue during a time when the staff was underutilized. The absence of opportunity costs of the staff working on these clients reduced the cost of serving them, perhaps making them more profitable than the firm's analysis showed. Other negative outcomes occurred as well. There was ill will in the community from the firm dropping clients, especially those in the nonprofit sector. The firm also signaled that it was not particularly interested in small- and medium-sized clients, even though such entities dominated the local community. When the firm later lost one of its large clients, it was unable to replace that revenue, and the size of that office declined significantly. This example demonstrates that an assessment of customer value must go beyond current profitability, and give consideration to capacity, seasonality of work, customer behavioral implications, public image, and other factors. As mentioned earlier, the first action after finding that certain customers are unprofitable or provide minimal profit is an attempt to make the customer more profitable. Only as a last resort should termination of the customer be considered.

# Upgrading Unprofitable Customers

Cokins observes that there are two elements of customer profitability: the mix of products and services that each customer purchases and the costs of providing various services to that customer.[8] A customer buying low-margin goods and services, and requiring a lot of individual customer service, is likely to be an unprofitable customer.

The goal of revenue management is to attempt to move such customers into profitable territory. The first element of customer unprofitability—buying low-margin products and services—may be addressed by:

- Raising prices;
- Adding new products and services, and possibly abandoning the least profitable ones; and
- Promoting higher-margin items to these customers.

The second element of customer unprofitability—requiring excessive special services—may be addressed by:

- Streamlining these services to reduce their cost;
- Adding extra charges for services above a certain threshold; and
- Offering a mix of services at varying prices.

Customer profitability is dynamic. An unprofitable customer today could become a very profitable customer in the future. Similarly, a customer's current profitable status could deteriorate. Monitoring customer profitability is an ongoing task, and continuing efforts are needed to enhance profitability of each customer.

# Conclusion

Successful revenue management is not about serving as many customers as possible, at any cost. Revenues *and* profits are the goal, both short term and especially long term. Having a customer information system that identifies many features of each customer's history and behavior is essential. Analysis of customer value then leads to determining which customers regularly contribute to profits and which do not. Finding ways to convert the customer's unprofitable status to profitable status then becomes the revenue management challenge.

# CHAPTER 12

# Making Revenue Management Decisions

Revenue management should be an intentional, high-level management activity. A company should have a portfolio of revenue management techniques that it employs, with some knowledge of the effectiveness of each. A good system of analyzing revenue management decisions and tracking and evaluating their results is essential to achieving revenue growth and greater profitability.

Michael Treacy, in his best-selling book *Double-Digit Growth*, suggests that many companies do not do a good job of managing revenue growth. Growth is not achieved by chance or luck, or by coming up with an occasional hot product, or by having a temporary surge of business.[1] Rather, it involves a four-part discipline of:

- Protecting the current customer base;
- Gaining market share from competitors;
- Finding and participating in the most attractive market segments; and
- Entering both adjacent markets and new markets.[2]

Many of the specific pricing and customer-gaining techniques discussed throughout this book are tactical means of achieving these broad goals.

Revenue management decisions may be made on a judgmental basis or may be based on complex models.

## Modeling and Revenue Management

A considerable literature exists on developing models of the revenue process for use in revenue management applications. The early applications by the airlines were based on extensive, detailed models of passenger data to identify flights where price reductions might increase overall revenue.

This book is not about modeling. Readers interested in modeling are referred to *The Theory and Practice of Revenue Management* by Talluri and Van Ryzin[3] and to numerous articles in the *Journal of Revenue and Pricing Management*. This literature is briefly highlighted in the following sections. According to Talluri and Van Ryzin, modeling for revenue management generally involves repeated applications of the following four steps:[4]

1. Data collection and analysis of historical prices, customer demand, and other causal factors.
2. Estimation and forecasting, which includes specifying and estimating explanatory variables for the demand curve, forecasting demand, and forecasting other relevant factors such as cancellation rates.
3. Optimization to determine the best prices, allocations, discounts, and the like.
4. Applying the optimization results to direct the sale of capacity or inventory via the transaction processing system.

Models can and should be formulated for a variety of revenue management decisions. Talluri and Van Ryzin identify three broad categories of such decisions:[5]

1. Structural pricing decisions, such as the following:
   a. Should list prices, negotiated prices, or auction prices be used?
   b. What basis should differentiation among customers be done, if at all?
   c. What terms (discounts, refund or cancellation rights, or other pricing concessions) should be offered?
   d. Should products or services be offered on a bundled or unbundled basis?
2. Specific pricing decisions, such as the following:
   a. How to set prices?
   b. How to vary prices across product or service categories?
   c. How to vary prices over time?
   d. When to offer discounts or markdowns?

3. Quantity decisions, such as the following:
   a. Accepting or rejecting offers
   b. Allocating capacity across products, product lines, or distribution channels
   c. Taking a product off the market

### Modeling in the Airline Industry

The airline industry is the original, and perhaps still the primary, practitioner of revenue management. There is an extensive literature on modeling in the airline industry. Early work by Kimes identified four factors that determine airline revenue management:

- Demand forecasting
- Overbooking policy
- Pricing
- Capacity allocation (also called seat inventory control)[6]

With the possible exception of overbooking, these factors would play a role in most revenue management models. Studying the rich literature on airline revenue management could provide modeling guidance for managers in other industries.

Unlike some applications of revenue management, such as restaurants or golf courses, airline (and hotel) models involve network considerations—multiple nights for hotels and multiple flights for airlines. While hotels can quote different prices for different nights, an airline ticket is commonly quoted as a single price, though outbound and return flights may be priced separately. Network models have been used to deal with flights having multiple legs and return flights that are not taken until some time after the outgoing flights. Modeling approaches have been developed for such applications.[7] Alliances among airlines, where *code sharing* is used to combine flights on multiple carriers, further complicate the task.[8]

As management modifies the operating characteristics of the business, traditional optimization techniques may be no longer applicable. The UK discount airline, bmi, changed to offering one-way, no-restriction fares, varying only the price over time. The decision thus became when to post a fare change during the time reservations for the flight were being received.[9]

Revenue management need not be a pure modeling activity. Research by Zeni showed that a human dimension adds to value.[10] Zeni found that adding an analyst, who would provide an element of decision making that is not reflected in the formal model, could add up to 3 percent in incremental revenue.

## Measuring the Success of Revenue Management

A good measurement system is essential to assessing the success of any activity. If revenue management is to be a long- term practice of the organization, measures to assess the success of this activity are needed.

One obvious measure is the growth of total revenue itself. But a second important consideration is that revenue growth should be profitable; hence, it is important to simultaneously consider both revenue *and* income growth.

What income measure is appropriate? Some suggest net income, while others suggest gross profit. Both have their merits. Gross profit (sales revenue minus the direct costs of providing the goods or services) addresses the question of how much additional value has been created by the revenue growth. Certainly, if increased revenues impose greater direct costs, the merit of generating those revenues is questionable, at least beyond the short term. But gross profit, at least as conventionally measured in accounting, may not capture all the costs incurred in growing revenue. To the extent that revenue growth is accomplished via increased promotion, greater sales effort, and the like, these costs typically are included in selling, general, and administrative (SGA) expenses and are not considered part of the gross profit. Also, if revenues are expanded by selling to less credit-worthy customers, losses from bad debts are not usually incorporated in gross profit. The recent experience in the mortgage industry attests to the significance of this consideration.

One approach is to try to isolate all the marginal effects of increased revenues—both direct and SGA. But separately identifying all these costs can be difficult or not cost-effective. A truly successful long-term revenue management activity should show improvement in all three measures: *total revenue, gross profit,* and *net income.*

An emerging field in accounting and finance is that of *sustainability.* Do the revenue management activities lead to a lasting impact on performance measures? While short-term, nonsustainable gains are certainly of some value, sustainable improvements are vital to the long-term health of the organization. Thus, effects on these three measures should be considered for both the short term and the long term.

Looking at overall measures of revenue, gross profit and net income may not provide enough information, especially when various revenue management techniques are employed. Some finer breakdowns need to be considered.

### Analyzing Revenue Sources

Understanding one's current revenue and its sources is a key starting point for revenue management. Some authors suggest preparing a *sources of revenue* statement, containing these five components:[11]

1. Continuing sales to existing customers;
2. Sales to new customers, which gain market share at the expense of competitors;
3. New sales by expanding one's markets, such as new geographical areas, new stores, Internet sales, expanded customer base, and the like;
4. Sales from moving into *adjacent* markets that build on the company's core capabilities; and
5. Sales from entirely new lines of business unrelated to previous core capabilities.

### Sales to Existing Customers

Existing customers constitute the company's revenue base. Retention of that base is a key to ongoing success. It is often said that it costs up to nine times more to gain a new customer than to keep an old customer. Metrics that help assess customer retention include calculation of the percentage of prior customers retained, and growth in sales to retained customers. This latter measure is akin to the *growth in same store sales* commonly reported in the retail industry.

The ability to continue to sell to existing customers depends on the nature of the business. A personal-injury law firm, for example, would not normally have continuing customers, as evidenced by their constant advertising to attract new customers. Other businesses may have repeat customers, but the repurchase cycle may be fairly lengthy: new car dealers, furniture stores, appliance dealers, and the like. Measuring customer retention in such businesses requires a longer than annual cycle.

Even when direct retention of customers is not expected because of the nature of operations, some businesses find that current customers may contribute to ongoing revenue generation by providing *referrals*. Thus, professional service providers such as attorneys and certified public accountants (CPAs); durable goods providers such as home builders and car dealers; and *one-time* service providers such as funeral homes, wedding planners, colleges, and the like, may track referrals as a way of indicating that their current customers are happy with them, even though those same customers do not continue to require their product or service. Indeed, *word of mouth* has long been considered to be the best advertising.

Thus, although *sales to existing customers* is a standard measure of performance, it depends on the nature of the business and the length of the repeat sales cycle, and it may include indirect repeat sales such as referrals by past customers.

Sales to New Customers

Sales to new customers may often be a goal of revenue management. As mentioned earlier, one way to acquire new customers enmasse is to acquire a competitor. In such a situation, retention of the acquired customer base is an especially critical concern. Apart from this strategy, there are many ways to add new customers. In its most limited form, new customer sales means adding new customers without expanding the company's existing base of operations, usually by added sales effort and promotion. However, the next category also involves sales to new customers, and it may not be feasible to differentiate the two.

### New Sales from Expanding Markets

Probably the most common way of adding new customers, apart from acquisitions, is to expand the company's market presence. This action may take the form of entering new geographic areas, including international markets; opening new retail outlets; finding new channels of distribution; and reaching out to potential customers by other means.

In retail businesses, opening new stores is a common approach. By knowing same-store sales, one can estimate the additional revenues brought about by opening new locations. New locations may take various forms. Coffee-and-donut shops, fast food operations, banks, and other providers have moved beyond free-standing locations, offering their products or services within supermarkets or discount stores, on college campuses, at rest stops on interstate highways, and even in megachurches. In some cases, satellite locations may even be nonattended, such as ticket-sale kiosks and ATMs. All these satellite locations, being smaller in scale, should be measured separately from free-standing operations. Because of the smaller volume of business and the possible higher costs of operating these satellite locations, the three-part measurement of revenue, gross profit, and net income should be used.

New channels of distribution are also a common way of expanding the customer base. Many businesses now have an Internet presence as well as physical locations. Internet sales are an expanded form of long-standing catalog sales. Internet sales offer considerable cost savings over catalogs, since printing and distribution costs become nonexistent.

### Sales from Adjacent Markets

This revenue source also builds on the existing core capabilities of the company and may overlap with the foregoing by moving into new markets for existing products and services. Adjacent markets often cater to the same customer base, as when a toy retailer adds children's clothing or a bookstore adds a coffee shop. Adjacent markets may utilize the same distribution system or the same production technology.

### Sales from New Lines of Business

Finally, new revenues may be generated by entirely new activities, unconnected to existing activities. The conglomerate movement some years ago was an extreme example, when companies pursued diversification so as to minimize cyclical effects. Considerable costs may be incurred when entering new lines of business. Here an acquisition of an existing business, in the desired new line, may be the most cost-effective way to enter new fields, rather than developing the expertise and infrastructure from the ground up.

It is important for companies to understand what percentage of total amount each of these categories contributes to the total revenue of the company. Each category may require a different strategy to manage or grow. Categorizing and quantifying revenue sources enable an organization to develop more accurate strategies for managing revenues.

### *Analyzing Revenues by Product Mix*

The previous discussion of revenue sources analyzes revenues primarily by market segment and customers, and to some extent by products and product lines. A simpler analysis focuses on product sales rather than customers, such as the following:

- Revenues from sales of existing products;
- Revenues from sales of revised products; and
- Revenues from sales of new products.

This approach seems most suitable for a company with a broad line of relatively stable products, where product upgrades and revisions occur from time to time, and where new products are often introduced. A food manufacturer, for example, could add products within each variety of a product line, such as new flavors or features of soft drinks (regular, diet, caffeine free, lemon flavored, etc.). Distinguishing a new product from a revised product may be difficult at times. For example, a new flavor of soft drink might be a revised product, whereas adding energy drinks or flavored waters might constitute new products.

## Conclusion

The main point of this discussion is that an understanding of where one's revenues come from is not only a key starting point for managing revenues but also a useful tool for assessing the success of revenue improvement initiatives. As discussed earlier, tracking the effects of revenue management decisions on revenue, gross profit, and net income is a must!

# CHAPTER 13

# Emerging Issues in Revenue Management

Revenue management is a dynamic field. As new products and services emerge and new business models are created, revenue management techniques develop to meet these challenges. In this chapter, we consider several of these: the sharing economy, mobile retailing, and new financial reporting standards for revenue recognition.

## The Sharing Economy

One emerging concept in recent years is the notion of the *sharing economy*. A sharing economy focuses on access to resources—products and services—rather than direct ownership or control of those resources. Some forms of nonownership have long existed. People rent their living quarters rather than own them, or lease their vehicles rather than buy them. There is not much sharing here, as single users have the resource for lengthy periods. Greater sharing of resources has also long existed, in the form of hotels, car rentals, equipment rental, tuxedo rentals, and the like. Traditionally, the providers are well-established businesses who provide use of resources on a broad scale. The more recent sharing economy differs in that there are many more providers, often individuals, who have goods or services they are willing to share with others. Social media and mobile communications facilitate exchange of information, and middlemen have emerged to handle the linkage between providers and users, and to bring some sort of order to the market. This trend, which seems to be accelerating, has implications for traditional providers of goods and services and their revenue management.

In 2011, *Time Magazine* recognized "sharing" as one of its "10 Ideas That Will Change the World."[1] Companies like Napster, Netflix, and

Zipcar were the initial leaders, but these were still large-scale organizations. eBay and similar sites allowed anyone to become a retailer. Soon the sharing movement extended to individuals, aided by facilitators such as Airbnb, which allowed people to rent living space to travelers; SnapGoods, which focused on renting goods such as power tools; and Uber, which facilitates ride sharing. Many of these function in localized communities, where the supplier and user are in close proximity.

There are many motivations for the emergence of the sharing economy. Many of one's possessions are used only rarely. For items that are expensive to purchase and have lengthy periods of idle time, an alternative to buy and own can become popular. As ownership of goods expands, storage space becomes a problem, especially in large communities where large living spaces are very expensive. If there were a convenient way to have access to something on the few occasions one needs it, that would save money, save space, and perhaps also contribute to the environment. From a provider's viewpoint, it is a chance to earn some extra income. The Internet, social media, and mobile communications helped make sharing a reality.

Several elements are needed for a sharing economy to function. Good information flow is needed, so that suppliers and users can readily identify each other. Ease of access is needed so that the exchange is quick and convenient. A matchmaking service helps to vet suppliers and customers, adding an element of trust to the system via ratings and reviews. The matchmaker may also enable a trustworthy payment system.

In the past several years, sharing has expanded rapidly. Short-term living accommodations and autos or rides have been two big markets, but sharing has expanded to many other areas as well: pet watching, boats and recreational vehicles, bicycles, power tools, outdoor gear, party supplies, musical instruments, and many others.[2] Almost anything can be shared. And sharing is not limited to physical goods. Sharing has entered the lending market via crowdfunding sites such as Kickstarter. Labor sharing is also increasing, as individuals delegate work to others via organizations such as TaskRabbit and as employers increasingly utilize temporary workers via such sites as Wonolo.[3]

Initially, the sharing economy poses a revenue threat for traditional businesses, whether sellers or renters of goods and services. Virtually any individual could now be a competitor, and matchmakers emerged to bring together these new suppliers and customers. While each new competitor was small, in the aggregate they could cause a significant drain on revenues. But these new business models are not without their problems and concerns. Issues of regulation have impacted the sharing of living space and of rides, as laws regarding occupancy and taxi service have often interfered. Issues of legal liability and insurance coverage also confront individuals offering to share goods and services.

Slowly, the sharing economy may change from being a threat to traditional providers to becoming an opportunity for increased revenue. For example, Zipcar, the hourly car-rental service, acquired a stake in Wheelz, a peer-rental firm, and in turn Zipcar was acquired by Avis, a traditional car-rental organization. Similarly, General Motors' affiliate GM Ventures invested in RelayRides, another peer-rental company, and facilitated access via its Onstar system, so that cars could be unlocked, started, and locked without keys, using an Onstar app.[4] If such trends continue, peer-to-peer sharing may become just another way traditional companies can provide their goods and services.

## The Mobile Retailer

Initially, traditional "brick-and-mortar" retailers were confronted with online retailers, which brought about major change in retailing. A good percentage of retail sales is now conducted online. "Brick-and-mortar" retailers have had to contend with the "showrooming" phenomenon, whereby customers would come to stores to examine and compare goods, and perhaps get technical advice, and then leave to make their purchase online, usually at a lower price.

Retail businesses where a significant element of service is involved have been much less affected by online sales. An emerging trend here is the use of mobile locations; food trucks have been a major example. This enables the retailer to easily change locations to where customers might be at a given time, such as events and festivals. Again, this development may pose a threat to the extent that new competitors emerge, or an opportunity if a traditional retailer adds this form of delivery.

Mobile retailing also offers an opportunity for retailers to bring their goods and services to small communities, where a permanent location may not be justified. One could envision a jewelry store or a men's wear store, for example, visiting a small community periodically, where it could not sustain a full-time location. At one time, public libraries brought "bookmobiles" to outlying communities. Beyond the emergence of food trucks, however, mobile retailing may be an opportunity waiting to happen.

## The Impact of Financial Reporting on Revenue Management

External financial reporting is a powerful driver of managerial action. Management is rightfully concerned about how its actions and decisions will impact its financial reports to investors and creditors.

The International Accounting Standards Board (IASB), which governs financial reporting in much of the world, and the Financial Accounting Standards Board (FASB), which governs financial reporting in the United States, recently issued a comprehensive new standard for revenue reporting. This standard replaces a variety of informal practices and special-industry standards that had accumulated over the years.[5]

The new standard is approaching implementation as this chapter is written. We discuss some of the possible effects of the new standard on revenue management. The actual effects will unfold over the next several years.

### Highlights of the New Standard

The new standard identifies a five-step process to guide the recognition of revenue:

1. Identify the contract with the customer.
2. Identify the performance obligations contained in the contract.
3. Determine the transaction price.
4. Allocate the transaction price to the performance obligations.
5. Recognize revenue when each performance obligation is satisfied.

There are two key concepts here: the notion of *contracts* with customers, and the idea of *performance obligations* under those contracts.

## Identifying Contracts

There are five conditions to the existence of a contract:

1. The contract is expected to change the risk and timing of the parties' future cash flows.
2. The parties have approved the contract and commit to satisfying their obligations under it.
3. Rights regarding goods and services to be transferred can be identified.
4. Payment terms can be identified.
5. The customer's intention and ability to pay make it probable that the seller will collect what it is entitled to.

A contract need not be written; it can be verbal, or even implied by customary business practices. Most business transactions should fit this broad definition of a contract.

## Performance Obligations and Revenue Management

Performance obligations are promises to transfer a distinct good or service, or a series of essentially similar goods or services. Performance obligations may be explicitly stated in a contract, or may be implied as a result of customary business practices or vendor policies. Performance obligations involve only the provisions of goods and services to the customer; they do not include internal business processes of the seller, such as billing.

One challenge is to identify when there are multiple performance obligations. Multiple obligations exist if the customer can benefit from each good or service on its own, and the vendor's promises are separately identifiable in the contract. For example, a contract to sell and install equipment usually involves two performance obligations, if the equipment could be purchased without installation or the installation could be performed by other than the equipment vendor.

The existence of multiple performance obligations requires that the transaction price be allocated, and each portion of the revenue be recognized as that performance obligation is satisfied. In the aforementioned example, part of the contract revenue would be recognized when the equipment is delivered, and part when installation is complete. But if the sale and installation are deemed to be a single performance obligation, no revenue would be recognized until installation is completed.

The focus on tying revenue recognition to the completion of each performance obligation has implications for the issue of bundling versus unbundling of goods and services. The more the goods and services are bundled into a single contract, the greater the challenge in allocating the recognition of revenue. Since most companies desire to recognize revenues as soon as possible, this may act as a disincentive to bundling.

### Transaction Price and Revenue Management

The third step in the aforementioned revenue recognition process is determination of the transaction price. This may initially appear straightforward, but it may not be. The transaction price is defined as the consideration the seller expects to receive, without regard to the customer's credit risk. That is, bad debts do not enter into the determination of the transaction price.

However, the existence of "variable consideration" does impact the determination of the transaction price. Variable elements of the transaction price include revenue management staples such as:

- Discounts
- Rebates
- Incentives
- Bonuses or penalties
- Price concessions
- Refunds and credits

Each of these should be considered in estimating the transaction price—the consideration the seller expects to receive. Some of these elements of variable consideration may be subject to change as circumstances evolve. For example, a contract containing bonuses or penalties for achieving or not achieving performance targets may use an expected value method or a most-likely method to estimate the transaction price. When multiple performance obligations are also involved, requiring the allocation of variable consideration to performance obligations, the process may indeed become difficult.

## The Future of Revenue Management

Revenue management is still in its early years as a separate discipline. It first emerged about 30 years ago, in the 1980s, as American Airlines sought to combat the threat of low-cost, low-price competitors. It succeeded in its initial limited goal. Revenue management then continued to be used as a means to maximize revenue on a short-term, service unit basis. The goal was to add paying passengers to each flight, ideally in ways that did not infringe on normal-price business. After a few years of aggressively applying these techniques, the chief executive officer (CEO) of American Airlines stated, "Yield management is the single most important technical development in transportation management since we entered the era of airline deregulation .... We estimate that yield management has generated $1.4 billion in incremental revenue in the last three years alone."[6]

Revenue management concepts then spread to other businesses with similar characteristics—perishable and substantially fixed service capacity, a heavily fixed cost structure, varying and uncertain demand, and some ability to forecast. Hotels, restaurants, golf courses, car-rental agencies, and other similarly positioned businesses soon began to apply these concepts. Much of the literature for the first 20 years or so focused on these industries.

Another movement, not initially identified as revenue management but having similar characteristics, arose in the aggressive pricing and promotion techniques of the automotive industry. *Rebates*, along with low-cost financing, became common elements of pricing in this industry, again designed to sell as much as possible of the output of a largely fixed-capacity industry. In a humorous takeoff on the rebate technique, a pizza shop in my neighborhood once sported a sign proclaiming, "Large cheese and pepperoni pizza, $209.99; $200 rebate."

The two flagship industries, airlines and automotive, despite being aggressive users of some form of revenue management, were not known for their overall success. Although they may have succeeded in growing revenue, they often could not do so profitably. The low prices designed to add extra customers to an existing base soon became the norm, and on an overall basis these prices were not profitable. This outcome was an early lesson that marginal-cost pricing might work at the margin, for a few extra sales, but it was not a viable approach for broad-scale pricing.

Despite these early cases of *winning the battle but losing the war*, revenue management is still with us over 30 years later. It has expanded well beyond its initial uses and emerged in a broader scale of applications, though it is still a developing field. Various writers proclaim that, despite its early limitations, the field has a bright future.

### Example of Evolution: The Hotel Industry

Robert Cross was one of the early writers to popularize the term *revenue management*. The cover of his 1997 book on the topic has a review excerpt from the *Wall Street Journal*: "Forget downsizing. As companies focus again on real growth, one emerging business strategy is 'POISED TO EXPLODE.'"[7] Twelve years later, Cross, Higbie, and Cross stated that "the era has ended when revenue management can stand alone as a tactical approach to room management."[8] Their article on a renaissance of revenue management talks of a rebirth of *profitable* revenue management (emphasis added). They report the results of interviews with 16 revenue management leaders from the hospitality industry.

A first point made is that revenue management can no longer be just a tactical approach to managing the room inventory. Initially, specialized pricing was based on the assumption that it could be limited to a small subset of customers, by establishing *rate fences*. But this attempt at limitation has not worked; especially in the Internet age, price information is readily and broadly available. Now revenue management has to consider the interaction of all the revenue streams in a hotel: rooms, food and beverage, meeting facilities, gift shops, parking, and so forth.[9] Consulting firms have arisen to offer revenue management guidance. For example,

IDeaS Revenue Solutions offers pricing and revenue management software, services, and consulting to the hospitality and travel industries.

## Trends and Directions

At the Second Annual Revenue Management and Price Optimization Conference in 2006, experts from more than 30 companies presented their views on the then-current state of revenue management. Some of the views, as reported by Garrow et al., included the following:[10]

- Some organizations are centralizing their pricing decisions and seek to align their sales incentives with their revenue and profit goals. In some cases, sales staff still has some pricing discretion, but sales incentives reflect margin as well as volume.
- In industries ranging from cruise lines to symphony orchestras, the emphasis is on defining and pricing an "experience," sometimes allowing customers to design their own package. This tactic aims to reduce the customers' focus on price alone and to make comparison shopping more difficult.
- Increased bundling of goods and services at a single price, again reducing the focus on price alone.
- Greater pricing parity across varying distribution channels, as the Internet has significantly increased the transparency of prices.

A subsequent conference focused on the transition from intuitive approaches to revenue management to analytical-based decisions.[11] Modeling techniques that were once employed primarily by airlines and hotels have become more widespread, and an increasingly broad range of companies have come to formalize the revenue management function in their organizations. An executive of Winn-Dixie supermarkets stated that, prior to 2005, the company "really had no formal strategy with respect to pricing, didn't really have a formal category management, didn't necessarily put the right types of items on sale, and so forth."[12] Now they and others are seeking to determine for which items discounting drives higher volumes of sales and for which items it does not.

# Conclusion

The field has grown from its initial rather narrow focus of *yield management*, seeking to fill a fixed, perishable capacity on a short-term basis to a richer, more broadly applicable discipline of *revenue management*, featuring an expanded range of techniques in much broader contexts.

The field continues to grow. It is suggested that the next iteration may be *demand management*, adding the creation and direction of demand to the present revenue management focus of managing current demand.[13] Demand management adds consideration of distribution channels, market segments, and customer relationships to the current concern with price management.

Whatever the future direction, it is clear that revenue management is here to stay. It is applicable across all types of organizations, and it merits inclusion as a focus of top management.

# Notes

## Chapter 1

1. Bouter (2013).
2. Cizaire (2014).
3. Huefner and Largay (2008), p. 245.
4. Porter (1985), p. 11.
5. Motta (1996), p. 1B.
6. Hymowitz (2001), p. C-5.
7. Pfeffer (2010).
8. Pfeffer (2010), p. 34.
9. Mass (2005).
10. Ertimur, Livnat, and Martikainen (2003); Swaminathan and Weintrop (1991).
11. Ertimur, Livnat, and Martikainen (2003).
12. Sidel and Enrich (2007).
13. "Coca-Cola Enterprises Inc. Reports Strong Start to 2004" (2004).
14. Shell (2009), p. 158.
15. Ton (2008), p. 22.
16. Marn and Rosiello (1992), pp. 84–85.
17. Treacy (2003), pp. 4–5.
18. Treacy (2003), pp. 8–9.

## Chapter 2

1. Cross (1997); Smith, Leimkuhler, and Darrow (1992).
2. Cross and Dixit (2005).
3. Kimes (2005a).
4. Kimes and Thompson (2004).
5. Kimes (2005b).
6. Biehn (2006).
7. Lieberman and Dieck (2002).
8. Kimes and Schruben (2002).
9. Billings, Diener, and Yuen (2003); Slager and Kapteijns (2003).
10. Freeland (2007).
11. Volpano and Bilotkach (2008).
12. Bain (2008).
13. Hawtin (2003).

14. Bain (2008), pp. 303–4.
15. Kuyumcu (2002).
16. Orkin (2003), pp. 172–4.
17. Karaesmen and Nakshin (2007).

## Chapter 3

1. Kimes (2005a).
2. Kaplan et al. (1990), pp. 20–21.

## Chapter 4

1. Phillips (2005), p. 25.
2. Buffalo Sabres (2014).
3. Holden and Burton (2008), pp. xviii–xix.
4. Holden and Burton (2008), pp. 51–55.
5. Marn and Rosiello (1992), p. 85.
6. An extensive discussion of price differentiation by customers can be found in Phillips (2005), Chapter 4.
7. Kapner (2014), pp. B1–B2.

## Chapter 5

1. Kapner (2013), pp. B1, B4.
2. Holden and Burton (2008), p. 2.
3. Dudley and Rupp (2013), pp. 21–22.
4. Ng and Banjo (2014), pp. B1–B2.
5. Shell (2009), pp. 112–113.
6. Shell (2009), p. 113.
7. Mutzabaugh (2010), p. 2B.
8. Anderson (2010a), p. 3.
9. Anderson (2010a), Chapter 2.
10. Anderson (2010b).
11. Anderson (2010a), pp. 20–29.
12. Marn and Rosiello (1992), pp. 86–87.

## Chapter 6

1. Kahneman, Knetsch, and Thaler (1986a).
2. Kahneman, Knetsch, and Thaler (1986a), p. S286.
3. Kahneman, Knetsch, and Thaler (1986a).

4. Kahneman, Knetsch, and Thaler (1986a), pp. S287–S288.
5. Kahneman, Knetsch, and Thaler (1986a), pp. S295–S297.
6. Güth, Schmittberger, and Schwarze (1982).
7. Many credit-card agreements preclude merchants from offering a different price for non-credit-card transactions, so such discounts are rarely seen.
8. Phillips (2005), p. 302.
9. He did ask us for documentation of when we signed up and how we knew of the discount. We understand that he subsequently complained to his travel agent, and did receive a discount voucher should he take another cruise.
10. Winer (1986); Kahneman, Knetsch, and Thaler (1986b).
11. McMahon-Beattie et al. (2002), pp. 31–32.
12. Anderson (2010b).
13. Phillips (2005).
14. Kahneman, Knetsch, and Thaler (1986b).
15. Bolton, Warlop, and Alba (2003).
16. Kimes and Wirtz (2003).
17. Shoemaker (2003).
18. Shoemaker (2003).

# Chapter 7

1. Anthony and Reese (1996).
2. Kaplan et al. (1990).
3. Kaplan et al. (1990), p. 17.
4. Kaplan et al. (1990), pp. 17–18.
5. Kaplan et al. (1990), pp. 4–14.
6. Kaplan et al. (1990), p. 14.
7. Huefner (2014), pp. 20–21.
8. Banker, Potter, and Srinivasan (2005).
9. Shields and Shields (2005).
10. Marshall (1890).
11. Parkin, Powell, and Matthews (2002), p. 84.
12. Phillips (2005), p. 45.
13. Parkin, Powell, and Matthews (2002), pp. 77–79; Phillips (2005), p. 45.
14. Phillips (2005), p. 46.

# Chapter 8

1. McNair and Vangermeersch (1998).
2. McNair and Vangermeersch (1998), pp. 226–234.
3. McNair and Vangermeersch (1998), pp. 114–122.

4. McNair and Vangermeersch (1998).
5. McNair and Vangermeersch (1998), p. 121.
6. Klammer (1996).
7. Klammer (1996), p. 15.
8. Klammer (1996), p. 44.
9. Klammer (1996), p. 43.
10. Huefner (2011).
11. Huefner and Largay (2013), p. 309.

## Chapter 9

1. Goldratt and Cox (1992), p. 301.
2. Adapted from a case prepared by Professors Sanford C. Gunn and Philip R. Perry, School of Management, State University of New York at Buffalo. Used with permission.

## Chapter 10

1. McNair and Vangermeersch (1998), p. 96.
2. McNair, Polutnik, and Silvi (2000), pp. 26–27.
3. McNair Polutnik, and Silvi (2000), p. 27.
4. The term comes from the gambling industry and designates what is needed to participate in the game. According to Wikipedia: *In business, table stakes also refer to the minimum entry requirement for a market or business arrangement. It can refer to pricing, cost models, technology, or other capabilities that represent a minimum requirement to have a credible competitive starting position in a market or other business arrangement. For example, if you want to be a wireless service provider, the table stakes are the basic features you need to have in order to be in that business to achieve foundation capability—network, handsets, a data service, a mail server, and the like. Beyond that, real competitive advantage comes from additional nimbleness and cost or product differentiation.*
5. Shell (2009).
6. Shell (2009), pp. 11–13.
7. Shell (2009), pp. 15–16.
8. Shell (2009), pp. 36–37.
9. Shell (2009), p. 162.
10. Holden and Burton (2008), pp. 76–78.
11. Holden and Burton (2008), p. 77.
12. Zeithaml (1988).
13. Dube and Shoemaker (1999).

14. Holden and Burton (2008), pp. 116–118.
15. Turbotax (2015).
16. Walt Disney World (2014). All prices are for ages 10 years and up; lower prices apply for children aged three to nine years.

## Chapter 11

1. Holden and Burton (2008), pp. 9–10.
2. Cooper and Kaplan (1991), p. 134.
3. Kanthal.com (2010).
4. Kaplan (1989a).
5. Kaplan (1989a), p. 3.
6. Kaplan (1989a), p. 5.
7. Kaplan (1989b), pp. 1–2.
8. Cokins (2013).

## Chapter 12

1. Treacy (2003), pp. 4–5.
2. Treacy (2003), pp. 16–17.
3. Talluri and Van Ryzin (2004).
4. Talluri and Van Ryzin (2004), p. 18.
5. Talluri and Van Ryzin (2004), p. 3.
6. Kimes (1989).
7. Côté, Marcotte, and Savard (2003).
8. Vinod (2005); El-Haber and El-Taha (2004).
9. Donnelly, James, and Binnion (2004).
10. Zeni (2003).
11. McCafferty (2004); Treacy (2003).

## Chapter 13

1. Walsh (2011).
2. *The Economist* (2013); *The Economist Technology Quarterly* (2013).
3. Scheiber (2014).
4. *The Economist Technology Quarterly* (2013).
5. Financial Accounting Standards Board (2014).
6. Robert Crandall, quoted in Smith, Leimkuhler, and Darrow (1992), p. 31.
7. Cross (1997), cover.
8. Cross, Higbie, and Cross (2009), p. 56.

9. Cross, Higbie, and Cross (2009), p. 56.
10. Garrow et al. (2006).
11. Garrow and Ferguson (2008).
12. Garrow and Ferguson (2008), p. 226.
13. Anderson and Carroll (2007).

# References

Anderson, C. 2010a. *Free: The Future of a Radical Price*. New York: Hyperion.

Anderson, C., and B. Carroll. 2007. "Demand Management: Beyond Revenue Management." *Journal of Revenue and Pricing Management* 6, no. 4, pp. 260–63.

Anderson, J. October 2010b. "Drive Time: More for Your Money." *Kiplinger's Personal Finance* 64, no. 10, p. 69.

Anthony, R.N., and J.S. Reese. 1996. *Baldwin Bicycle Company*. rev. ed. Cincinnati, OH: South-Western College.

Bain, J. 2008. "Future of Revenue Management—From the Plane to the Shelf." *Journal of Revenue and Pricing Management* 7, no. 3, pp. 302–6.

Banker, R.D., G. Potter, and D. Srinivasan. 2005. "Association of Nonfinancial Performance Measures with the Financial Performance of a Lodging Chain." *Cornell Hotel and Restaurant Administration Quarterly* 46, no. 4, pp. 394–412.

Biehn, N. 2006. "A Cruise Ship Is Not a Hotel." *Journal of Revenue and Pricing Management* 5, no. 2, pp. 135–42.

Billings, J.S., A.G. Diener, and B.B. Yuen. 2003. "Cargo Revenue Optimisation." *Journal of Revenue and Pricing Management* 2, no. 1, pp. 69–79.

Bolton, L.E., L. Warlop, and J.W. Alba. 2003. "Consumer Perceptions of Price (Un)Fairness." *Journal of Consumer Research* 29, no. 4, pp. 474–91.

Bouter, E.-J. 2013. *Pricing: the Third Business Skill: Principles of Price Management*. Loenen aam de Vecht, The Netherlands: FirstPrice BV.

Buffalo Sabres. December 10, 2014. "2014–15 Individual Game Tickets." http://sabres.nhl.com/club/page.htm?id=39501

Cizaire, C. 2014. "Book Review: Pricing: The Third Business Skill: Principles of Price Management." *Journal of Revenue and Pricing Management* 13, no. 4, pp. 339–40.

"Coca-Cola Enterprises Inc. Reports Strong Start to 2004." April 28, 2004. Dow Jones Newswire. http://ir.cokecce.com/phoenix.zhtml?c=117435&p=irol-newsArticle&ID=1345242&highlight

Cokins, G. 2013. "Turning Bad Customers Good." *CGMA Magazine*, December 04. http://www.cgma.org/magazine/features/pages/20137267.aspx (accessed December 26, 2013).

Cooper, R., and R.S. Kaplan. 1991. "Profit Priorities from Activity-Based Costing." *Harvard Business Review* 69, no. 3, pp. 130–35.

Côté, J.-P., P. Marcotte, and G. Savard. 2003. "A Bilevel Modeling Approach to Pricing and Fare Optimisation in the Airline Industry." *Journal of Revenue and Pricing Management* 2, no. 1, pp. 23–36.

Cross, R.G. 1997. *Revenue Management: Hard-Core Tactics for Market Domination.* New York: Broadway Books.

Cross, R.G., and A. Dixit. 2005. "Customer-Centric Pricing: The Surprising Secret for Profitability." *Business Horizons* 48, no. 6, pp. 483–91.

Cross, R.G., J.A. Higbie, and D.Q. Cross. 2009. "Revenue Management's Renaissance: A Rebirth of the Art and Science of Profitable Revenue Generation." *Cornell Hospitality Quarterly* 50, no. 1, pp. 56–81.

Donnelly, S., A. James, and C. Binnion. 2004. "bmi's Response to the Changing European Airline Marketplace." *Journal of Revenue and Pricing Management* 3, no. 1, pp. 10–17.

Dube, L., and S. Shoemaker. 1999. "Loyalty Marketing and Brand Switching." In *Handbook of Services Marketing and Management*, ed. T. Swartz. Beverly Hills, CA: Sage.

Dudley, R., and L. Rupp. 2013. The Perils of Price-Matching. *Bloomberg Businessweek.* May 13–19, pp. 21–22.

*The Economist.* 2013. "The Rise of the Sharing Economy," May 9.

*The Economist Technology Quarterly.* 2013. "All Eyes on the Sharing Economy," May 9.

El-Haber, S., and M. El-Taha. 2004. "Dynamic Two-Leg Airline Seat Inventory Control with Overbooking, Cancellations and No-Shows." *Journal of Revenue and Pricing Management* 3, no. 2, pp. 143–70.

Ertimur, Y., J. Livnat, and M. Martikainen. 2003. "Differential Market Reactions to Revenue and Expense Surprises." *Review of Accounting Studies* 8, no. 2–3, pp. 185–211.

Financial Accounting Standards Board. 2014. Revenue from Contracts with Customers (Topic 606). FASB Accounting Standards Update No. 2014-09, May 2014. Norwalk, CT: Financial Accounting Standards Board.

Freeland, L.C. 2007. "Adoption of Customer-Centric Cargo Revenue Management: Brief History of Cargo Revenue Management vs. Passenger Revenue Management." *Journal of Revenue and Pricing Management* 6, no. 4, pp. 284–86.

Garrow, L., and M. Ferguson. 2008. "Revenue Management and the Analytics Explosion: Perspectives from Industry Experts." *Journal of Revenue and Pricing Management* 7, no. 2, pp. 219–29.

Garrow, L., M. Ferguson, P. Keskinocak, and J. Swann. 2006. "Expert Opinions: Current Pricing and Revenue Management Practice Across U.S. Industries." *Journal of Revenue and Pricing Management* 5, no. 3, pp. 237–47.

Goldratt, E.M., and J. Cox. 1992. *The Goal: A Process of Ongoing Improvement.* Great Barrington, MA: North River Press.

Güth, W., R. Schmittberger, and B. Schwarze. 1982. "An Experimental Analysis of Ultimatum Bargaining." *Journal of Economic Behavior and Organization* 3, no. 4, pp. 367–88.

Hawtin, M. 2003. "The Practicalities and Benefits of Applying Revenue Management to Grocery Retailing, and the Need for Effective Business Rule Management." *Journal of Revenue and Pricing Management* 2, no. 1, pp. 61–8.

Holden, R.K., and M.R. Burton. 2008. *Pricing with Confidence: 10 Ways to Stop Leaving Money on the Table.* Hoboken, NJ: John Wiley & Sons.

Huefner, R.J. 2011. "A Guide to Integrating Revenue Management and Capacity Analysis." *Management Accounting Quarterly* 13, no. 1, pp. 40–46.

Huefner, R.J. 2014. "An Introduction to Revenue Management: Exploring Common Techniques and the CPA's Role." *The CPA Journal* LXXXIV, no. 6, pp. 17–21.

Huefner, R.J., and J.A. Largay III. 2008. "The Role of Accounting Information in Revenue Management." *Business Horizons* 51, no. 3, pp. 245–55.

Huefner, R.J., and J.A. Largay III. 2013. "Identifying Revenue Opportunities via Capacity Analysis." *Journal of Revenue and Pricing Management* 12, no. 4, pp. 305–12.

Hymowitz, C. 2001. "Using Layoffs to Battle Downturns Often Costs More Than It Saves." *Wall Street Journal,* July 24, p. C–5.

Kahneman, D., J.L. Knetsch, and R.H. Thaler. 1986a. "Fairness and the Assumptions of Economics." *Journal of Business* 59, no. 4, part 2, pp. S285–S300.

Kahneman, D., J.L. Knetsch, and R.H. Thaler. 1986b. "Fairness As a Constraint on Profit Seeking Entitlements in the Market." *American Economic Review* 76, no. 4, pp. 728–41.

Kanthal.com. October 5, 2010. http://www.kanthal.com/about-us

Kaplan, R.S. 1989a. *Kanthal (A).* Cambridge, MA: Harvard Business School.

Kaplan, R.S. 1989b. *Kanthal (B).* Cambridge, MA: Harvard Business School.

Kaplan, R.S., J.K. Shank, C.T. Horngren, G. Boer, W.L. Ferrara, and M.A. Robinson. 1990. "Contribution Margin Analysis: No Longer Relevant/ Strategic Cost Management: The New Paradigm." *Journal of Management Accounting Research* 2, pp. 1–32.

Kapner, S. 2013. "Black Friday: A Retail Illusion." *The Wall Street Journal,* November 26, pp. B1, B4.

Kapner, S. 2014. "Lines Blur Between Outlets and Regular Stores." *The Wall Street Journal,* October 13, pp. B1–B2.

Karaesmen, I.Z., and I. Nakshin. 2007. "Applying Pricing and Revenue Management in U.S. Hospitals—New Perspectives." *Journal of Revenue and Pricing Management* 6, no. 4, pp. 256–59.

Kimes, S.E. 1989. "Yield Management: A Tool for Capacity-Constrained Service Firms." *Journal of Operations Management* 8, no. 4, pp. 348–63.

Kimes, S.E. 2005a. "A Strategic Approach to Yield Management." In *Yield Management: Strategies for the Service Industries,* eds. A. Ingold, U. McMahon-Beattie, and I. Yeoman. 2nd ed. London, England: Thomson Learning.

Kimes, S.E. 2005b. "Restaurant Revenue Management: Could It Work?" *Journal of Revenue and Pricing Management* 4, no. 1, pp. 95–7.

Kimes, S.E., and G.W. Thompson. 2004. "Restaurant Revenue Management at Chevys: Determining the Best Table Mix." *Decision Sciences* 35, no. 3, pp. 371–92.

Kimes, S.E., and L.W. Schruben. 2002. "Golf Course Revenue Management: A Study of Tee Time Intervals." *Journal of Revenue and Pricing Management* 1, no. 2, pp. 111–20.

Kimes, S.E., and J. Wirtz. 2003. "Perceived Fairness of Revenue Management in the U.S. Golf Industry." *Journal of Revenue and Pricing Management* 1, no. 4, pp. 332–44.

Klammer, T. ed. 1996. *Capacity Measurement & Improvement: A Manager's Guide to Evaluating and Optimizing Capacity Productivity.* Chicago, IL: Irwin Professional.

Kuyumcu, A.H. 2002. "Gaming Twist in Hotel Revenue Management." *Journal of Revenue and Pricing Management* 1, no. 2, pp. 161–67.

Lieberman, W.H., and T. Dieck. 2002. "Expanding the Revenue Management Frontier: Optimal Air Planning in the Cruise Industry." *Journal of Revenue and Pricing Management* 1, no. 1, pp. 7–24.

Marn, M.V., and R.L. Rosiello. 1992. "Managing Price, Gaining Profit." *Harvard Business Review* 70, no. 5, pp. 84–94.

Marshall, A. 1890. *Principles of Economics.* London, England: Macmillan.

Mass, N.J. 2005. "The Relative Value of Growth." *Harvard Business Review* 83, no. 4, pp. 102–12.

McCafferty, J. 2004. "Testing the Top Line: Analyzing a Company's Sources of Revenue Can Bring Insights into Growth." *CFO Magazine*, October 1. no. 3, pp. 89–91.

McMahon-Beattie, U., I. Yeoman, A. Palmer, and P. Mudie. 2002. "Customer Perceptions of Pricing and the Maintenance of Trust." *Journal of Revenue and Pricing Management* 1, no. 1, pp. 25–34.

McNair, C.J., L. Polutnik, and R. Silvi. 2000. "Outside-in Cost and the Creation of Customer Value." *Advances in Management Accounting* 9, pp. 1–41.

McNair, C.J., and R. Vangermeersch. 1998. *Total Capacity Management: Optimizing at the Operational, Tactical, and Strategic Levels.* Boca Raton, FL: St. Lucie Press.

Motta, M. 1996. "Growth Takes Over as Corporate Focus." *USA Today*, June 5, p. 1B.

Mutzabaugh, B. 2010. "All-You-Can-Fly Passes Return for Fall Travel." *USA Today*, August 18, p. 2B.

Ng, S., and S. Banjo. 2014. "Wal-Mart gets stuck in a 'diaper arbitrage'." *The Wall Street Journal*, July 24, pp. B1–B2.

Orkin, E. 2003. "The Emerging Role of Function Space Optimization in Hotel Revenue Management." *Journal of Revenue and Pricing Management* 2, no. 2, pp. 172–74.

Parkin, M., M. Powell, and K. Matthews. 2002. *Economics.* Reading, MA: Addison-Wesley.

Pfeffer, J. 2010. "Lay off the Layoffs." *Newsweek*, February 15, pp. 32–37.

Phillips, R.L. 2005. *Pricing and Revenue Optimization.* Stanford, CA: Stanford Business Books.

Porter, M.E. 1985. *Competitive Advantage: Creating and Sustaining Superior Performance.* New York: Free Press.

Scheiber, N. 2014. "Corporate America Is Using the Sharing Economy to Turn Us into Temps." *The New Republic*, November 23.

Shell, E.R. 2009. *Cheap: The High Cost of Discount Culture.* New York: Penguin Press.

Shields, J.F., and M.D. Shields. 2005. "Revenue Drivers: Reviewing and Extending the Accounting Research." *Advances in Management Accounting* 14, pp. 33–60.

Shoemaker, S. 2003. "The Future of Pricing in Services." *Journal of Revenue and Pricing Management* 2, no. 3, pp. 271–79.

Shoemaker, S., and R.C. Lewis. 1999. "Customer Loyalty: The Future of Hospitality Marketing." *Hospitality Management* 18, no. 4, 345–70.

Sidel, R., and D. Enrich. 2007. "For Citi, Cost-Cutting Is Only Half the Battle." *Wall Street Journal*, April 12, p. A3.

Slager, B., and L. Kapteijns. 2003. "Implementation of Cargo Revenue Management at KLM." *Journal of Revenue and Pricing Management* 3, no. 1, pp. 80–90.

Smith, B.C., J.M. Leimkuhler, and R.M. Darrow. 1992. "Yield Management at American Airlines." *Interfaces* 22, no. 1, pp. 8–31.

Swaminathan, S., and J. Weintrop. 1991. "The Information Content of Earnings, Revenues, and Expenses." *Journal of Accounting Research* 29, no. 3, pp. 418–27.

Talluri, K.T., and G.J. Van Ryzin. 2004. *The Theory and Practice of Revenue Management*. Boston, MA: Kluwer Academic.

Ton, Z. 2008. "The Hidden Risk in Cutting Retail Payroll." *Harvard Business Review* 86, no. 2, p. 22.

Treacy, M. 2003. *Double-Digit Growth: How Great Companies Achieve It—No Matter What*. New York: Penguin Group.

TurboTax. 2015. "Personal Tax Products and Services." http://turbotax.intuit.com/personal-taxes (accessed January 16, 2015).

Vinod, B. 2005. "Alliance Revenue Management." *Journal of Revenue and Pricing Management* 4, no. 1, pp. 66–82.

Volpano, L.J., and V. Bilotkach. 2008. "A Case Study: How to Rationalise Concert Entertainment Ticket Pricing." *Journal of Revenue and Pricing Management* 7, no. 1, pp. 3–6.

Walsh, B. 2011. "Today's Smart Choice: Don't Own, Share." *Time*, March 17.

Walt Disney World. 2014. "Tickets & passes." http://disneyworld.disney.go.com/tickets-passes (December 10, 2014).

Winer, R.S. 1986. "A Reference Price Model of Brand Choice for Frequently Purchased Products." *Journal of Consumer Research* 13, no. 2, pp. 250–56.

Zeithaml, V.A. 1988. "Customer Perceptions of Price, Quality, and Value: A Means-End Model and Synthesis of Evidence." *Journal of Marketing* 52, no. 3, pp. 2–22.

Zeni, R. 2003. "The Value of Analyst Interaction with Revenue Management Systems." *Journal of Revenue and Pricing Management* 2, no. 1, pp. 37–46.

# Index

## OTHER TITLES IN THE MANAGERIAL ACCOUNTING COLLECTION

Kenneth A. Merchant, University of Southern California, Collection Editor

- *Sustainability Reporting: Managing for Wealth and Corporate Health* by Gwendolen B. White
- *Business Planning and Entrepreneurship: An Accounting Approach* by Michael Kraten
- *Breakeven Analysis: The Definitive Guide to Cost-Volume-Profit Analysis* by Michael Cafferky and Jon Wentworth
- *Corporate Investment Decisions: Principles and Practice* by Michael Pogue
- *Drivers of Successful Controllership: Activities, People, and Connecting with Management* by Jurgen Weber and Pascal Nevries
- *Revenue Management in Service Organizations* by Paul Rouse, William McGuire, and Julie Harrison
- *Revenue Management: A Path to Increased Profits* by Ronald Huefner
- *Cost Management and Control in Government: Fighting the Cost War Through Leadership Driven Management* by Dale Geiger
- *Setting Performance Targets* by Carolyn Stringer and Paul Shantapriyan
- *Strategic Cost Analysis* by Roger Hussey and Audra Ong
- *Customer-Driven Budgeting Prepare, Engage, Execute: The Small Business Guide for Growth* by Floyd Talbot
- *Value Creation in Management Accounting: Using Information to Capture Customer Value* by CJ McNair-Connolly, Lidija Polutnik, Riccardo Silvi, and Ted Watts
- *Breakeven Analysis: The Definitive Guide to Cost-Volume-Profit Analysis, Second Edition* by Michael E. Cafferky and Jon Wentworth
- *Effective Accounting for Small Business: A Guide to Business and Personal Financial Success* by David E. Tooch

# Announcing the Business Expert Press Digital Library

*Concise e-books business students need for classroom and research*

This book can also be purchased in an e-book collection by your library as

- a one-time purchase,
- that is owned forever,
- allows for simultaneous readers,
- has no restrictions on printing, and
- can be downloaded as PDFs from within the library community.

Our digital library collections are a great solution to beat the rising cost of textbooks. E-books can be loaded into their course management systems or onto students' e-book readers. The **Business Expert Press** digital libraries are very affordable, with no obligation to buy in future years. For more information, please visit **www.businessexpertpress.com/librarians**. To set up a trial in the United States, please email **sales@businessexpertpress.com**.

CPSIA information can be obtained
at www.ICGtesting.com
Printed in the USA
LVOW13s1316010217
522874LV00019B/525/P